BACHELORS

BACHELORS

*The Psychology of Men
Who Haven't Married*

Charles A. Waehler

Westport, Connecticut
London

Library of Congress Cataloging-in-Publication Data

Waehler, Charles A.
    Bachelors : the psychology of men who haven't married / Charles A.
Waehler.
       p.   cm.
    Includes bibliographical references and index.
    ISBN 0-275-95668-7 (alk. paper)
    1. Bachelors—Psychology. I. Title.
HQ800.3.W34 1996
155.6′422—dc20   96-21323

British Library Cataloguing in Publication Data is available.

Library of Congress Catalog Card Number: 96-21323
ISBN: 0-275-95668-7

First published in 1996

Praeger Publishers, 88 Post Road West, Westport, CT 06881
An imprint of Greenwood Publishing Group, Inc.

Printed in the United States of America

The paper used in this book complies with the
Permanent Paper Standard issued by the National
Information Standards Organization (Z39.48-1984).

10 9 8 7 6 5 4 3 2 1

CONTENTS

Contents

ACKNOWLEDGMENTS

Personal goals are rarely achieved without others' assistance. This is certainly the case for me; without the intellectual, emotional, and personal support of a whole cadre of essential people this book would not have been written. On these pages I wish to continue the process of thanking the many people who have helped with various facets of conceptualizing, configuring, and building this book.

Special thanks go first to all the bachelors who shared their lives and stories with me. Your cooperation served as the foundation for my activity. I treasure the fact that you stretched yourselves to accommodate me; I hope our collaboration has been mutually beneficial.

Several individuals helped transform this material from disjointed article reviews, interviews, and test data into more interwoven stories of men's development. They deserve acknowledgment as teachers, mentors, and guides: Lee Blum, Jack Crites, Sonny Cytrynbaum, Margaret Lee, and Bill Parker.

The following people read drafts and offered meaningful feedback, which helped energize my efforts and shape this presentation: Craig Earnest, Linda Edelstein, Rosalie Hall, Sue Hardin, Shannon Herman-Saxon, Rich Lenox, Wendi Maurer, Linda Subich, and Jane Williams.

I appreciate George Zimmer of Psychotherapy Press for helping me find my way to the Greenwood Publishing Group. While at Greenwood I have benefitted from the wise consult and editorial acumen of James Sabin. Thanks, too, to Marc Harari for his help with the final manuscript production.

I am also grateful to members of my immediate family: Mom; Dad and Marilyn; Pixie and Paul; Janie and Bill; Jon and Erin; you have served as indispensable guides and companions throughout my life. "Family" also extends beyond relatives. As this book has developed, I have benefitted from the loving support of Fran Birndorf, Anne Contant, Craig Earnest, Eve and Mark Epstein, Mark Hilsenroth, Paul Levy and Sylvia Chinn-Levy, and Dean and Sheila McIntire.

Finally, I am grateful and indebted to Linda Edelstein, an essential person in my support system during this entire project. You consistently help me play, work, and grow, all elements necessary to have my spirit sing. Thank you.

1

BACHELOR STEREOTYPES

"Old Bachelor" is a card game to replace "Old Maid." The Old Bachelor combs his hair over his bald spot, keeps his mother's picture on his dresser, and has a thick "little black book." He is more pitiable than attractive. The two Chicago-area women who produced the game were tired of the clichéd Old Maid as an ugly, long-nosed, fearsome woman who makes you a loser if you get stuck with her. They created their bachelor image by surveying the prevailing attitudes about bachelors. Both games highlight the negative image of singleness, but the "Old Bachelor" version begins to even the score between the sexes by drawing on some of the deeply rooted and popularly held views of bachelors. Are these beliefs reasonable? To what extent does their characterization accurately reflect the true bachelor nature?

First let's clarify what is meant by the term *bachelor* in this psychological inquiry: Bachelors are heterosexual men who are at least age 40 and have never married. Some descriptions use less stringent criteria for qualifying bachelors and include any man not currently married. For instance, divorced or separated men are sometimes considered bachelors instead of being more accurately described as single men. Other observers do not consider sexual orientation and include homosexual men in the bachelor ranks. Age must also be a criterion for defining someone as a bachelor: No one would argue that a 15-year-old should be counted among the bachelor population. It is unfair to call individuals who have not *yet* married "never-married," as they may become married in their future: A 25-year-old who is not yet married is still likely to do so. However, by age 40 the reverse is true—men (and women) who are not married by age 40 are not likely to ever marry. By age 40 only one bachelor in five will marry, and census and research data suggest that by age 45 the odds increase to about 1 in 20 (U.S. Bureau of the Census, 1993). Therefore, setting 40 years of age as the time when men really become bachelors makes sense.

An accurate understanding of bachelors is more critical now because there are more bachelors today than at any other time in America's history. There are currently over 3.1 million men who are at least 40 years old and have never been married. And the number is increasing. There are more single men in their early twenties because men are marrying later: The average age of a man marrying for the first time is 26.5 years, the highest it has been in a hundred years. This age has increased steadily since 1956, when the average age at first marriage was 22.5 years. Since 1975 alone this age has risen three full years (U.S. Bureau of the Census, 1993). There are now more bachelors in their forties because when men delay marriage, they become more likely to never marry.

Since most men are married by age 27, a man who has not married by this age becomes different from the norm. Bachelors at age 40 are even more dissimilar because 90 percent of men have gotten married at least once by then (U.S. Bureau of the Census, 1993). But what are never-married men like? They obviously behave differently when it comes to marriage. What are they like emotionally? Socially? Do they view marriage with contempt or longing? What do we know about these men who choose to forge a life so different from those of their peers? Surprisingly little. And what we do "know" about bachelors is probably more steeped in myth, folklore, and fable than reality.

CREATING EXPLANATIONS

As humans we are wonderfully curious about ourselves and others. We wonder about people close to us and about people we only remotely hear about. We inevitably compare our own paths with theirs. We construct explanations to satisfy our interests.

Bachelors evoke curiosity, and people naturally formulate their own pet theories:

> "Uncle Bill never married because he had to take care of his ailing parents."
>
> "Alan was never the same after watching his parents' ugly divorce."
>
> "Paul loved someone years ago, but was too much of a workaholic to ever marry."
>
> "Steve had everything going for him. Why should he settle down?"
>
> "Larry must have been gay because he never married."

Such declarations can become stereotypes and beliefs about a whole class of people without ever examining the merits of the observations.

Not knowing can be disturbing, so people often create beliefs about unrequited love, early traumatic experiences, or homosexuality to explain the phenomenon of men not marrying. These beliefs, true or not, have flourished because there is a lack of plausible, proven, scientific explanations to replace them. Never-married adults have not been studied as intensely as their married peers. This is due to the relatively small percentage of bachelors, especially in the past, and to the fact that psychologists and sociologists overlooked them because they assumed bachelorhood was temporary; these factors combined to create a collective blind spot. (For example, "Reasons for *Failing* to Marry" is the major section heading of a textbook about marriage that is in its sixth edition.) Although there has been introductory research in recent years, the longstanding lack of hard data has perpetuated myths and fantasies about the single adult.

Some of the popularly held stereotypes present never-married men in a positive light. Having negotiated life without a partner, bachelors may exemplify the American ideal of a rugged, swaggering, self-sufficient man. Would Captain James T. Kirk of the USS *Enterprise* inspire the same devotion from millions of fans if he had gone on his voyage accompanied by his wife and children? Probably not.

One of the strongest images we maintain collectively is of the single man who is independent and not tied down to any particular, possibly mundane, lifestyle. Positive bachelor myths respect their choice and admire them for choosing a singular path different from that of the majority of their peers. Successful single men earn full credit for their accomplishments because they have not had a "good woman" behind them. Bachelors have the flexibility to quit a job or start a new business without worrying about the potential problems this might unleash on their families. Having the freedom to pick up and go anywhere when they choose and not having to sacrifice for a wife, children, and in-laws are other enviable advantages. With readily available birth control and the increase of non-marital sex, bachelors can also have the sexual advantages of marriage with none of the responsibilities.

These positive descriptions may be enticing to a woman involved with a bachelor. There is relief that he doesn't bring a lot of old "baggage" with him. She does not have to worry about making a good impression on his kids or living with financial constrictions from his divorce. She could also look forward to the fact that she does not have to introduce him to her friends—and her mother—as divorced or "coming out of a bad marriage."

However, glamorous portraits of minority groups are rare, and this is also true about bachelors. The overriding public sentiment toward never-married men is disapproval. Popular myths cast the never-married man in a dubious light; prevailing stereotypes about never-married men are grim. A middle-aged, heterosexual man who has never married evokes a stream of disapproving images, including

- womanizer
- woman hater
- marriage hater
- mama's boy
- nerd
- narcissist
- sexual deviant
- immature person
- miser
- workaholic

Even in the most positive popular images—those of delaying marriage until being professionally secure or being a playboy—never-married men carry with them overtones of immaturity, selfishness, lechery, and social irresponsibility. The prevailing beliefs about why people do not marry can be summarized as follows:

- They are hostile toward members of the opposite sex or are homosexual.
- They are immature, unwilling to assume responsibility, neurotic, or emotionally fixated on a parent.
- They are unattractive or unhealthy.
- They have failed in the dating game either because they are socially inadequate or because they are fixated on a lost love.
- They are overfocused on economics, either perceiving themselves as too poor to marry or perceiving marriage as a threat to their careers.
- They are just unluckily isolated by geography, education, or occupation.
- They are driven to make a political statement against marriage or maintain some sort of "principled deviance" (Cargan & Melko, 1982, pp. 18–19).

Bachelors are not alone in being criticized. In fact, the stereotype that singles are weird may apply even more to women. The traditional view is that women are "saved" by marriage, gaining families and financial security. A woman who cannot "get" a man must be a loser. Attitudes still prevail that women are made "whole" through marriage and "complete" through parenting. (It is only lately that women are in positions to ensure their own financial security—even more recently some single women are having children or adopting them.) Therefore, single women are usually pitied, disliked, or ascribed a low status—except when they are needed, as in times of war. Hurtful terms such as *spinster* and *old maid* are applied to women who do not marry. People are suspicious as to why they were not "good enough" to "catch" a husband. Historically, though, in spite of these condemnations single women have been more acceptable than single men; demographically there are more adult women than adult men at all ages, and the social custom of men marrying younger women has meant that there are always "extra" women.

Another social custom is that men do the proposing, so they control their marital fate. These factors contribute to the idea that there is something drastically "wrong" with bachelors—they must be really dreadful if they lose at the marriage game.

Disregarding the prevailing myths for a moment, three potential portraits of bachelors are possible. At one extreme, never-married men could be strong, independent, and self-determining. A second, middle-ground portrait to emerge could be one of never-married men who are not particularly different from their married friends except for legal matrimony. At the other extreme, never-married men could be pathetic, weak, troubled, and pitiable. The fact that the negative portrait has prevailed reflects a need to see bachelors as contemptuous, oppositional, and abnormal, perhaps because the unmarried pose a threat to the choice made by the vast majority. Negative beliefs about the unmarried reassure the married that they made the right decision. Pitiable attributes attached to bachelors also represent society's need to deal with pervasive ambivalent feelings about commitment. We have a love/hate relationship with the notion of commitment. Americans value strength, personal independence, and self-reliance in men, but at the same time want every man to make a personal commitment to a woman and to promise to be forever faithful. The mixed messages are readily apparent. One way to resolve the irreconcilable differences is to make one position appear less desirable. This is what happens to the aging bachelor. Although praise, admiration, and allure are ascribed to some bachelors in the early part of their lives, as they age even this glamour withers.

BACHELOR IMAGES RECEIVING MASS ATTENTION

A quick look at political and other public figures reveal how bachelors who are treated with envy and admiration when they are young and treated suspiciously as they age. Prince Charles of Great Britain was "the world's most eligible bachelor"—a sought-after, prize catch, who dated a lot of women throughout his twenties and into his thirties. The media and the public enjoyed every moment. However, remaining single too long led to his being described as aimless, idiotic, or childish—we questioned whether he lacked "solid" credentials. As public contempt for Prince Charles grew, marriage was needed not only to guarantee heirs to the throne, but also to protect his reputation. The world would have treated him badly had he not married. The fact that his choice was the lovely 19-year-old Diana further enhanced his image. In some ways he was forced to wed, which might have contributed to his marital problems.

John F. Kennedy was in a similar position of not being taken seriously within political circles until he married. Although a bright, young politician, Kennedy had to leave behind his "reckless" youth, or further political prospects would have been unavailable. One point marking his transition into maturity and legitimacy was his marriage at age 36. Although many accounts say that his sexual behavior did not change when he wed, marriage and family were essential to his success. Kennedy yielded to pressure to "get with the program" by marrying, and he parlayed having a socially prominent wife and children into a real asset. There is a temptation to say that marriage as a requirement for legitimacy resides in the past, that society is more tolerant today. While this might be true, it will be interesting to see what happens to President Kennedy's son, John Kennedy, Jr., a bachelor who is affectionately regarded now, at age 35, as a potential young politician who is "sowing his wild oats."

Although these men are celebrities who have special demands and privileges, corporate America has similar requirements. Stories of single people being passed over for promotion abound. Married men "have what it takes," while single men are considered unreliable or less substantial. One study that surveyed 50 major corporations found that, although the official corporate position was that marriage was not essential to upward mobility, over 60 percent of executives surveyed reported that single executives tend to make snap judgments, and 25 percent said that singles are less stable than married people (Jacoby, 1974). Another popular belief is that bachelors will achieve less because they lack the home-based incentive to be successful.

These simplistic views of never-married men as outsiders who are odd or "just don't get it" are reinforced by the entertainment industry. A perceptive display of how bachelors differ from married men is seen in the movie *The Fabulous Baker Boys*. Jeff and Beau Bridges portray brothers, who make up a musical duo. Jack is the cynical "little brother" who smokes and drinks too much, carouses, irresponsibly offends booking agents, and does not follow through on commitments. In contrast, Frank responsibly manages the musical group, drives a station wagon, and mends the fences his brother has torn. Guess which of them is the bachelor with the rented apartment and which is the family man with a house in the suburbs. The differing world views of these two men lead to many fights. Eventually Jack's seduction of their vocalist leads to the duo's demise.

Inspector Morse of the PBS "Mystery" series is another man whose bachelor status is used to define his role to the public. In one introduction of his character hostess Diana Rigg describes him as "a man who has always been unconventional. He has never been comfortable with authority and is willing to break rules. He is indifferent to the rules, sometimes breaking them. Although he is a man of strong emotion, he has difficulty expressing it."

Cliff Claven, an ever-present character perched on a bar stool in the hit sitcom "Cheers," is another well-known case in point. An emotionally fragile nerd who was a virgin into his 40s while living at home with his mother, "Cliffie" is a fictional smorgasbord of the myths about bachelors. Cliff is an individual to be laughed at by television viewers and his fictional friends alike. His weirdness at his post-office job has almost reached legendary status as his coworkers retell stories about his antics. His friends at Cheers are fond of poking fun at him, but he continues to whine on with inconsequential trivia. In one memorable program he joins them in making up insulting "Mr. Claven's brain" jokes. Demonstrating how peculiar he is with women, the show's writers catch a laugh by having this mid-forties man give a devilish smile of delight when he peeks down the cleavage of a wooden ship's masthead.

Equally eccentric was Lieutenant Howard Hunter of the long-running "Hill Street Blues" series. The writers had no problem putting this bachelor into bizarre scenarios. For instance, he was a man controlled by many obsessions, including a peculiar commitment to cleanliness, order, and ritual. He was fascinated with guns, paranoid about seeing communist conspiracies, and hateful toward minorities. Though a meritorious officer, Howard often got into trouble with authority, resulting in his demotion for insubordination. Despondent about what he saw as a shameful act, Howard attempted suicide, although he botched the job. He made poor business decisions, once spending six figures on an assault vehicle, only to have it stolen when he left the keys in it, and trying to sell his friends on a condominium settlement built underground to survive thermonuclear war. His relations with women were out-

landish at best. Formal in all his interactions, Howard was especially uncomfortable around women, once nervously crushing a
champagne glass in his hand when being propositioned. His sexual
naiveté was even more apparent when he became intimately
involved with a transvestite man, a fact that even after sexual
activity had to be pointed out to him by a fellow cop.

Though Jack Baker, Inspector Morse, Cliff Claven, and Howard
Hunter are fictional portrayals, real-life bachelors, at least those
who make headlines, seem to also be cast in a suspicious light.
Ralph Nader is a wild-eyed, burning zealot. Warren Beatty was a
sleazy rake until he became a father and married. Jack Nicholson
is still an enigma in spite of his having become a father. Democratic
presidential nomination seeker and former California Governor
Jerry Brown is known as "Governor Moonbeam." Supreme Court
Justice David Souter is monastic and austere. When Justice Souter
appeared for confirmation hearings before the Senate Judiciary
Committee in September of 1990, some beliefs and expectations
about him were based on his bachelor status. For instance,
Newsweek wrote:

> Souter has come to be known as a decent if drab ascetic, a 50–year-
> old man from rural, white New England who has never married, never
> had children, never really been part of the modern America that
> constitutional law must necessarily confront. . . . Does Souter's de-
> tachment show someone with a special capacity to judge or does it
> reflect a stale mind and a narrow heart? (Kaplan & Cohn, 1990, p. 32)

A major concern among the committee members was whether this
man of slight physique and reticent demeanor could understand
the anguish of a woman facing an unwanted pregnancy. Attention
of this nature had never been focused on married justices.

Bachelors themselves may help perpetuate the negative myths.
Many bachelors think there is something wrong with a man who
does not marry. Although some never-married men are secure and
pleased with their choice, many have grave doubts and wonder if
something is wrong with them.

CLINICAL QUESTIONS ANSWERED SCIENTIFICALLY

The study on which this book is based offers some preliminary
understanding about the mystery of bachelors. The bottom line is

that stereotypes about never-married men appear to be largely simplistic and inaccurate. Just as it would be impossible to make reliable statements about all people who have chosen to get married, the bachelor caricature falls well short of reality. The stories that follow will shed light on the psychological functioning of this growing segment of the population.

There is *some* truth to all three of the competing portraits of never-married men, but real bachelors are much more complicated than their caricatures. Never-married men show some common characteristics, but also manifest a variety of complex individual personalities, which they bring to day-to-day activities. Therefore, in order to understand the psychology of never-married men and their choices, we will explore similarities *and* differences. It would be convenient if a single portrait could be painted, but sweeping generalizations and stereotypes provide weak and inaccurate representations of the diverse human spirit. Like their married counterparts, never-married men are individuals. However, bachelors have at least one decision in common—to not marry. This book looks at their conscious and unconscious psychological profiles, their experiences within their families of origin, their relationships with women, their development through adulthood, and their beliefs about marriage in order to demonstrate patterns that led to and maintain their being single.

This study generated typologies and descriptions of the common traits and unique characteristics of the individuals involved. Rich illustrations give vitality to the observations underlying the psychological theory as the men tell their own stories. In addition to examining the personal anecdotes of these men, applying practical psychological principles and a personality assessment instrument provides insight into the internal processes and personality structures of these individuals. Integrating other research with the Rorschach inkblot test and personal interview data provides insights that complement and lend clarity to the underlying dynamics of their individual stories.

My desire to examine the lives of never-married men was not conceived in a laboratory. My clinical involvement with a variety of men (as well as my wondering about my own choices) was the driving force behind research with this population. As a therapist I am engaged with people's very real ordeals as they struggle to work through their own issues. Certain specific therapeutic relationships gave rise to my scientific inquiry into bachelors. Carol, a mid-30s woman, was frustrated that her relationship with a never-married man was stagnant and dull. Jerry, a handsome, late-20s man, was feeling different from his friends as they all married. While he had deep concerns that he was not ready to make this kind of commitment, he also agonized over the plight of men who did not follow a traditional time line toward marriage. Having the most impact among my counseling experiences, however, was the memorable statement a client made during his brief encounter with psychotherapy. Ben, a 43-year-old bachelor, had been brought (perhaps dragged is a better word) into counseling by his girlfriend of four months, Jill. Ben was by all accounts an unremarkable individual: average height, a little portly, balding forehead, and probably good at his job as an electrician. He was not used to deep thinking or feeling. Although usually an easygoing person, Ben entered the second (and last) session of therapy rigidly, as if he were working hard to hold something inside. As the session got under way, I was trying to use this session to help Ben understand Jill's tears as she stated: "Can't you see, if you don't talk to me we can't continue this relationship." Ben's face remained emotionless as he responded, "Maybe it's best that we go our own way." Jill tried again: "But you will miss me, my company, the sex, when I am gone." Ben stayed with the conversation, but ended the relationship, by firmly making a most revealing and descriptive statement: "Maybe I will, but even a rat chews off his own leg if he is caught in a trap."

This painfully graphic statement communicated a great deal about Ben. It spoke to his need for freedom and how he felt this relationship was affecting him. His statement also exposed the lengths to which he would go in order to extricate himself from the trapped feeling he had. By characterizing himself as a rat, he also showed how inadequate he viewed himself to be within this relationship.

Ben's statement crystallized my need to know more about never-married men and their experiences. Scientist/practitioners like myself generate hypotheses and hunches from general notions about individuals and then confirm, modify, or reject these notions by consulting published scientific studies available in the vast array of journals in the field of human studies. To my dismay I found the collection of high-quality studies about never-married individuals to be extremely limited, so I undertook my own original studies.[1]

What my research has led me to conclude is that Ben's feelings, though extreme, are not so dissimilar to those experienced by many never-married, middle-aged men. Usually a man satisfied with his competence, Ben did not know how to interact with this woman. He accepted her initial overtures, but remained passive. Ben's statement about the "trap" of being with Jill conveyed his true feelings about the nature of relationships. Like many never-married men, Ben's high need for self-reliance and autonomy placed severe restrictions on his ability to become deeply committed to a woman. He was also stating that he would go to great lengths—even hurting himself and those around him—to remain free.

Ben's assertion captures some of the psychological elements of bachelorhood. However, he is an example of only one segment of the never-married population that was revealed in the study conducted and that will be explored fully in this book. Ben represents men who desire to be alone, find comfort in limiting outside stimulation, and stay away from others to protect themselves from being overwhelmed. These men are detached, but satisfied with their lives. They are not likely to change because the personality style that makes them singletons is deeply entrenched in all their undertakings. They are comfortable with their decision and become threatened only when they feel their privacy is in peril.

There are other satisfied never-married men who share Ben's need for individuality, but who are less emotionally rigid, are more comfortable with women, and therefore have relationships that last longer than Ben and Jill's four months. These men also show patterns of not being open with their feelings, but they are less threatened by interpersonal relations and do not regress to feeling like rats when they are involved with women. Frank, a 44-year-old, never-married man earning in the low six figures as a commercial real estate broker, describes himself as a bachelor

> because marriage has always been irrelevant to me. I have been in several relationships, very important and serious ones, with some very wonderful girls, but marriage was always just over the next hill, and we never got there. Well, I should say we never got there together; most of my old girlfriends have gotten there with someone else. I've always had too much else going on.

Frank, like Ben, has carved out a comfortable life for himself alone. Although not a very emotional person, he likes competing and achieving personal successes that he can call his own. He is glad to be unencumbered by children and jokingly, but revealingly, describes himself as being "single, solvent, and safe." Having moved to Chicago from Boston means that Frank misses having his old friends around, but he does little to overcome this distance. Instead, he withdraws from dealing with his real desire to be around boyhood and college friends by not dwelling on these feelings. Overall, however, Frank states that "I really have a lot more things to be thankful for than things I would like to change."

Less content with themselves and more disturbed by their limited ability to join in a committed relationship with a woman is the third type of bachelor: the group of conflicted men who are dissatisfied with their marital status. These men are conflicted about their very real, competing desires to have their independence and autonomy, and yet to have their own family. What stops them? Their personality style. These men have drifted into being middle-aged and never-married because of their patterns of being strongly individualistic and making a commitment to work for their own welfare. They show patterns of not being strongly assertive. Instead, they muse and mull over their decisions—particularly when emotions are involved. These men have many excuses, what they would call reasons, for not being married. Steve speaks to the underlying insecurity that some ambivalent bachelors feel as he wonders, "What if you get married and then someone better comes along?" Wayne also gives voice to his uncertainty as he frets that "you can't really trust that everything is going to work out, and because I have never been in a secure job, I'm not sure I could provide for the two of us." Conflicted men vacillate between wanting to be married and withdrawing from the demands that this would place on them. By not asserting themselves, they tend to have many personal needs that go unmet. Many of them seek psychotherapy to try to sort out the opposing messages they hear from within. The girlfriend who is driven crazy by a bachelor is probably with a conflicted man who flip-flops in his view of marriage, and she feels strung along until she cannot take it any more. She will leave the relationship hurt and, most damaging, blaming herself for not having found the key that could keep them together.

WHAT UNDERSTANDING PROVIDES

Understanding the deep experiences of our lives brings a measure of security, if not happiness. This book is written with the objective of understanding the psychology of bachelors and their relationships. Confirmation that knowledge helps came to me in a letter sent by a woman who read an early report in the *New York Times* (Blakeslee, 1991) on some of my research about never-married men. She wrote:

> I have recently separated from my long term companionship with a bachelor—we were involved for 10 years and lived together for the past four. After reading the article, I felt 50% better than I've felt for a long time. Although intellectually I feel I've done the right thing for myself and my future, emotionally and physically, I've really been having a hard time of things. Your report is helping me to realize that maybe it wasn't anything that either of us did or did not do that got us to this point but rather, circumstance and my former partner's personality, that was shaped long before I met him, that was actually to blame. You sounded exactly as if you were writing about him! There are so many similarities and character traits that I recognize.

While the increased understanding that this woman received did not transform her relationship, it seems to have gone a long way to heal her wounds.

Accurate information can mend psychological distress. Popular stereotypes—which portray bachelors with disapproving, unfavorable, and sometimes pitying overtones—do not fully perform this service. Although the work underlying this book has the limitation of being about a circumscribed, highly educated sample of white men from the midwestern United States, it provides an understanding and an explanation that are fuller than others currently available. Although not every bachelor will be accurately described in this book, the stereotypes about bachelors are exposed as overly simplistic. Bachelor images are more fully delineated here in order to overcome the disservice stereotypes perform by reducing a complex, heterogeneous group to a few pat adjectives and undeveloped descriptors. At the same time the publicly held observations, as will be seen, do carry some truth with them.

NOTE

1. The details regarding the methodology and parameters used for these studies are provided in three professional presentations: C. A. Waehler. (1995). Relationship patterns of never-married men and their implications for psychotherapy. *Psychotherapy*, *32*, 248–257; C. A. Waehler. (1991, August). Personality characteristics of never-married men. [A poster presentation at the Annual Convention of the American Psychological Association, San Francisco, CA]; C. A. Waehler. (1992, August). Mid-life adjustment of never-married men. [A paper presentation at the American Psychological Association, Washington, DC]. Copies of these materials are available from the author.

2

MEN, MARRIAGE, AND MENTAL HEALTH

Bachelor stereotypes lead most people to ask, "What is *wrong* with these guys? Why *can't* they marry?" However, these questions are equivalent to "When did you stop beating your wife?": They assume abnormality and misconduct. If we approach bachelorhood with questions that presuppose peculiarity or deviance or failure, the answers are inevitably self-protective or defensive. Instead, if we begin in a spirit of understanding bachelors with an open, non-judgmental interest, the question becomes "What are bachelors like?" Without making presumptions, the inquisitive mind reasons, "Bachelors are alike in not marrying, but what other common characteristics might they also have?" Serious research also considers that there might be diversity among bachelors and seeks to portray them with a variety of descriptors. Rather than painting the entire group with one quick, broad stroke, fine attention paid to individual differences and personal nuances can lead to sensitive representations.

The truth is that significant research regarding bachelors and their psychological makeup would diminish stereotypes—we would know real people, and our reactions would include more than distant, distorted suspicion. When we accumulate and inte-grate the combined work of other scientists, we gain insight into the men behind the simple Captain Kirk, Cliff Claven, and Don

Juan caricatures. However, only a smattering of purposeful work in psychology and sociology is available to date.

The large, general demographic studies that have examined mental health and marital status converge on one important point: Single men, as a group, are less well adjusted than their married counterparts. Indeed, studies of the incidence and prevalence of psychological distress consistently find the highest rates reported among unmarried individuals. One landmark study in this area (Gove, Hughes, & Styles, 1983) found that marital status is a more powerful predictor of mental health than education, income, age, race, or childhood background. Another review (Johnston & Eklund, 1984) concluded that married people are better adjusted than single people because married people suffer less mental disorder, are more free of depression caused by life stresses such as economic hardship, and report greater happiness. In addition, studies show that married men and women of all ages have a longer life expectancy than single persons. Although some studies say single people are similar emotionally to their married peers, *no* studies report single people as mentally healthier than married people.

These observations are rather damning. The talk-show mentality of pop psychology usually draws two quick and simple conclusions from these data. One is that marriage is a panacea: It protects married people from mental illness. The second knee-jerk conclusion is that bachelors are psychological losers, and hopefully these men who cannot commit will keep to themselves. However, both these judgments are potentially erroneous and could lead to dangerous prescriptions for a couple of reasons.

First, these studies tend to group together *all* unmarried individuals, even though we have many reasons to assume separated, divorced, and widowed people are quite different from never-married individuals. What gets ignored is that bachelors may be spared the disruptions, upset, and strains of being separated, divorced, or widowed. In fact, a National Institute of Mental Health study documents the tumult brought on by a failing relationship by concluding that the single most powerful predictor of stress-related physical and emotional illness is marital disruption (Pearlin & Johnson, 1977). Reports of men under psychiatric care show the lowest rates for married men and the highest numbers for separated and divorced men. Never-married and widowed persons fall somewhere in between (Gotlib & McCabe, 1990).

The second flaw linking marriage and mental health is that demographic surveys do not explain why an association exists or which factor causes the other. What we have is a simple correlation. However, an observed connection does not establish causality. For instance, there is a high correlation between teen dating and teen pregnancy, but dating does not necessarily *cause* pregnancy. The quick and simple conclusion that dating explains why pregnancy occurs ignores a lot of essential steps along the way. And yet people still conclude that not marrying causes psychological distress in singles without considering that there is a lot more going on there, too. This faulty reasoning that marriage is a cause or a cure for mental health has a long history dating back to the ancient Greek physician Hippocrates, who prescribed marriage, and its comfortable lifestyle and sexual satisfaction, as a cure for overly emotional women.

LINKING MARRIAGE TO MENTAL HEALTH

Three distinct theories have been proposed to explain why marital status is linked to mental health.[1] Only one of these theories implicates non-marriage as causing psychological problems, and even then some of these reasons are tangential.

The first explanation is that married people use psychological services less often than do unmarried people, so we assume they are healthier. According to this idea, called the *utilization* hypothesis, single and married individuals are equally healthy and unhealthy, but single people are counted as having greater suffering because they are more likely to seek professional treatment. Married people have families that provide support. In addition to using psychological services less often, married individuals are less likely to be admitted for hospitalization and are more likely to be released sooner to the care of their families (Robertson, 1974). What we do not know is whether the higher rates of hospital admission and the longer stays represent real differences in mental health, an accurate appraisal of available support, or hospital personnel's bias of presuming that married people have more substantial support networks.

The utilization theory assumes that the great potential for marriage to provide a solid social network to its participants is achieved, and that networks of caring affiliations are not available to single people. Psychological services are used more because they compensate for something lacking in the bachelor's life. The built-in social networks available to married people include spouse, children, and extended families. According to this hypothesis marriage uniquely offers reliable, consistent access to caring others. Indeed, bachelors' strong commitment to independence and self-reliance, as will be described in the next chapter, may leave them isolated from others in times of need. However, it may be that single people's social support networks are not recognized as legitimate by mental health personnel, and this fact could lead to more prescriptions for professional psychological services.

The second idea posed for the link between marriage and mental health, the *causation* explanation, proposes that marriage protects people from psychological distress. According to this reasoning, the increased social, emotional, and economic support available from a spouse and an extended family protects married people from life demands. Singles, on the other hand, have increased stress because of their unconventional social status. Some stressors may be more external; for instance, relying on only one paycheck or having fewer family members with whom to consult about life problems. But hassles may also cut deep to the bachelors' psyche. Because single men are viewed as deviants, unstable and incomplete, society may contribute to their psychological deterioration. The identity of single people may be damaged by the lack of acceptable social definition and support for their lifestyle. Married people may enjoy a "role" with meaning and value ascribed to it, but singles have the more difficult task of forging their own path.

The causation model is important in understanding singles because it implies that bachelors can be driven into mental illness because of the conditions of being unmarried. What does marriage offer that might protect its participants? What qualities does marriage have that explain its insulating effect? Psychologically protective marital qualities seem to fall into four categories: validational, functional, social, and cultural.

Validational qualities of marriage have to do with the love, respect, and honor marital partners promise each other. People need to be valued by others, to be affirmed, in order to develop positively. To be loved and to love are major building blocks of marital union that seem to be less available in other parts of today's society. Psychologist Carl Rogers spoke eloquently about the need to be *prized* by another human being (although he felt that marriage, with its conditions and constrictions, was not the best way to achieve this goal). Feeling a sense of personal worth and being treated with dignity and respect—elements presumed in marriage—are part of maintaining personal mental health, as well as being components of the cure for psychological problems.

Functional qualities in marriage have to do with managing life's daily tasks. One example is that in marriage many day-to-day tasks can be more effectively handled through a healthy distribution of labor: One partner takes responsibility for the laundry, while the other does the yardwork, or one takes responsibility for paying the bills, while the other focuses more on maintaining social ties. A good distribution of labor on the homefront ensures that each person's talents are maximized. Or for those increasingly rare couples that can afford to do so, you can still have a traditional division of labor, wherein one person makes money and one manages other life tasks. *All* single people have two jobs: breadwinner and homemaker. The added burden is obvious. In addition, economies of scale can be achieved in marriage. For instance, you only need one toaster, coffee maker, furnace, phone, refrigerator, and so on whether you live alone or with another. For some people a virtue of marriage comes from the cognitive gains they make: Better personal decisions can be made in dialogue with a spouse than would be reached in solitude. The ability (need?) to consult, which is built into a marriage, can lead to novel, more constructive choices. Lastly, and an important factor, economic responsibilities can be shared through the partnership of a marriage: Two paychecks can be combined into one pool of funds. Conversely, if economic hardship sets in, married people have twice the resources if they need to borrow money from their families.

Social gains are also possible in marriage. A readily available, stable, and reliable social network can be provided through marriage. Married people living together have consistent access to a significant person in their life. Married people, sometimes for better, sometimes for worse, have people to come home to and talk with. But not just any person. A spouse is presumably invested in your development and shares some of your goals. In addition, the familiarity that comes with marriage means that each spouse has reference to his/her mate's history. He or she also knows and can be sensitive to personal strengths and vulnerabilities. The significant knowledge and shared history possible in marriage offer tremendous potential for deep affection. Beyond affiliation married people also have a physical outlet available to them. For some people this virtue has to do with establishing a healthy sexual outlet, while others have less of a need for orgasmic delight, but do feel vital through close physical proximity to another person.

Cultural qualities provided by marriage include our belief that to be married is to be normal. Some people get married to avoid feeling aberrant. Getting married becomes like joining a club to which almost all adults belong. Most people's parents belong (or did belong at some time) to this club, so marriage serves as a way to enhance this identification, too. Marriage may serve many people's need to fit in. Being married helps give them an important role to play. For other people marriage serves as a rite of passage into adulthood. In addition, in our culture it is still normal (and best) to have children within a caring family, so marriage carries with it the opportunity to raise children successfully. Generativity is a strong human desire, which psychologists like Erik Erikson call an essential human need that searches for expression.

Beyond these major prerogatives, not being coupled can feel awkward and limiting. We live in a society built around the theme of "with's" (Davis & Strong, 1980). People go *with* people to parties and sit *with* people in restaurants. A person sitting alone in a movie theater is viewed suspiciously: Single women may be seen as pathetic wallflowers; single men may be seen as perverts and/or predators. People who approach others for information or conversation are better received if they are *with* someone else. Being *with* friends assists in overcoming uncomfortable situations. These social practices put special demands on the single person's ability to interact with his/her environment. And, as is so often the case, the rich get richer. That is, it is easier to make friends if you already have friends. Sociologist Margaret Adams suggests that "neighborliness is a basic prerequisite for everyone's social security, [but] for single people it is a categorical imperative to compensate for their lack of formally ascribed companionship and the support that is normally supplied through marriage or other dyad relationships" (Adams, 1981, p. 221).

So, according to the causation theory, because single people lack the validational, functional, social, and cultural qualities of marriage, they suffer more mental distress and seek more professional psychological relief. However, one assumption of this theory is that these protective qualities are available exclusively through marriage. Not considered is the idea that at least some of these attributes might be achieved by single individuals. A second assumption of the causation theory is that marriage's potential rewards always occur. Unfortunately the bottom line on many people's marital balance sheets shows them to be in the red: The advantages gained do not outweigh the prices paid. Remaining single may mean that although the possibilities are missed, the disappointments and struggles are also avoided. The descriptions of personality styles in the next chapters will explain how some bachelors have either achieved these important qualities through alternative means or navigated life without them.

The third explanation behind the link between marital status and mental health is that single people are less well adjusted to begin with, and that is why they do not marry. This *selection* theory proposes that the sifting process performed by the dating game selects psychologically disordered men out of the marriageable ranks. Even if a bachelor is eager to marry, according to this theory he is consistently rejected from the marriage pool because of psychological illness and will end up single. In this way the bachelor ranks are swollen by men who lack the social and psychological tools to get married: They may be unassertive, less bright, socially inept, psychologically handicapped, or suffer from personal adjustment problems. These limited men are less likely to marry, and if they do marry, they are more likely to divorce. Bachelors will show more psychological disorders throughout their lives because they were different to begin with.

The only way to demonstrate the selection theory and show bachelors as having certain psychological disturbances early in life that differentiate them from men who get married would be to take a huge group of boys and study them as they age to see who marries and who does not. Unfortunately these longitudinal studies are few and far between because they are complicated, expensive, and time consuming.

STUDYING BACHELORS DIRECTLY

The studies about bachelors that do exist report that gross psychological shortcomings or emotional illness is not exaggerated among bachelors. Bachelors as a group are not pathetic, nor are they psychologically inept. One study reports that "never-married men show no evidence of marked neurotic tendencies" (Halligan, 1980, p. 581). Another concluded that "there is no evidence that persons who live alone are selected into that living arrangement because of preexisting psychological problems, noxious personality characteristics, or incompetent socioeconomic behavior" (Hughes & Gove, 1981, p. 48). These studies counter the theory that disturbed men are selected out of marriage and into bachelorhood. On the other hand, particular, consistent personality patterns have been observed among bachelors and will be detailed in the chapters that follow. However, these psychological dispositions are neither exceptionally abnormal nor necessarily pathological.

Another important factor to examine about the selection hypothesis is whether socializing factors help determine which men become bachelors and which get married. The question here is "What conditions in society might direct certain types of men toward or away from marriage?"

Some demographers implicate our society's general belief in the superior position of the male as playing a hand in selecting fragile men into bachelorhood. They observe a natural order in which a man should be taller than a woman, he should be older than his partner, and a woman should "look up" to her husband. Sociologists call this process the "marriage gradient" (Bernard, 1972).[2] Marriages that conform to this hierarchy are more comfortable for the partners and for the people around them. By and large both men and women tend to marry mates with the same general class and cultural background, "but within that common background, men tend to marry women slightly below them in such measurable items as age, education, and occupation, and, presumably, in other as yet unmeasurable items as well" (Bernard, 1972, p. 33). One result is that men at the "bottom of the barrel" (in terms of marital qualities like mental health) have no one to marry: With no one to look up to them they are selected into the bachelor ranks. (Conversely, since there is no one for "top" women to look up to, the most superior women are the ones who never marry.)

One interesting study by Jon Darling (1981) examined the socializing process by looking at the lives of men who married for the first time when they were over 35 years old. He concluded that bachelorhood is primarily a situational, as compared to a psychological, condition. He suggests that bachelors are not basically different *types* of men, but men who have had unusual social histories. His interviews revealed that as adolescents these bachelors were typically involved with families or "significant others" who insulated them from the usual peer pressure to date. For example, after adolescence they remained in social settings, such as the priesthood, where marriage was not defined as important or appropriate for them. These men were deeply committed to their families, to their careers, or to friendships that fulfilled their needs. Any "serious" relationships that did develop were generally left to drift; marriage was generally not considered. As long as the men were comfortable with their situations, they were not likely to seriously seek a change such as marriage. These men did not expect to marry early, and their significant relationships with women were sparse. Indeed, many of the bachelors were not at all sexually active during large parts of their single lives.

Never-married men who married after age 35, Darling observed, did so as a result of changes in their social situations (e.g., friends moving away or the loss of a parent) and during personal turning points (e.g., career shifts or job transfers). These turning points were marked by "a pattern in which old situations broke down, old patterns of meanings became reworked, and stabilized relationships with significant others came to be interrupted to make way for new ones" (Darling, 1981, p. 26). Among his late-marrying sample the timing of the events was more important than the events themselves. Men married when they felt particularly vulnerable and/or were encouraged by a significant other. Most of the late-marrieds had short courtships; they were ready for marriage and took the opportunity when one developed.

Darling (1981) notes that as these men reached marriageable age, their lives were organized around other concerns such as developing a career or caring for aging parents. However, he also observed that these circumstances are not unique to bachelors.

> Some men, after all, marry *and* care for their aging parents at the same time or marry in the midst of active professional careers. Thus, the events in bachelors' lives may not differ significantly from those in the lives of men who marry early, but *the timing, definition, and perception of those events seem to vary considerably between the two groups. This produces and sustains important differences in identities, commitments, and consequent career patterns.* (p. 36)

These findings support the contention that non-marriage (or late marriage) may be due primarily to situational conditions rather than conditions that develop because of abnormal personality traits. His study points to the importance of analyzing a person's social context: "Continued singlehood or marriage, as any social state, develops as the end point of a series of situational contingencies, turning points, and commitments" (Darling, 1981, p. 35). Darling hoped his study would correct stereotypes and improve understanding of the relationship between society and the individual. He succeeds in broadening the focus of marital-choice investigations to look more at the socializing agents. Chief among these is the earliest and most significant social system for all people: their family.

Looking at the family of origin as determining future marital decisions considers that early experiences provide the foundations for the person's expectations, attitudes, and behaviors with respect to courtship, marriage, and family living. For example, persons whose parents' marriage ended in divorce or who had poor relations with their mothers or fathers may be less likely to marry as adults. The suspicion that parental relationships may have something to do with marriage choices goes a long way back in the mythology of marital relationships. "The most general association is that parents (or the mother in the case of the male) have been too possessive or protective. Thus, males who do not marry and often those who get divorced are perceived as 'mama's boys' " (Cargan & Melko, 1982, p. 70). Several good studies have helped begin to clarify the family of origin's influence on singlehood.

The stability of the parents' marriage may seem to provide a direct connection between a boy's experience and his subsequent decision about marriage. However, findings suggest that the presence or absence of an intact family of origin is not in itself directly related to remaining single. "Rather, other factors must be considered such as the cause of disruption and the type of family environment which replaces the original intact family" (Spreitzer & Riley, 1974, p. 539). Not surprisingly it is the *quality* of personal relations in the family during childhood that is associated with later marriage rates. Among men, poor relationships with mother, father, and siblings were associated with subsequent singlehood. Divorced or intact families are not important per se; rather, it is "the age at which the disruption took place, the cause of the disruption, and the type of reconstituted family in which the person was reared" (Spreitzer & Riley, 1974, p. 541).

One researcher was surprised to find only two differences in the original families of 100 married versus 100 single men (Rallings, 1966). The first difference associated with not marrying was that many of their families were somehow disgraced or stigmatized. A home was considered "disgraced" if either parent was an alcoholic, had been in prison, had a reputation for infidelity, or had a poor credit rating. The second difference was that bachelors were more likely to have grown up in a family where the father had a work schedule different from other fathers in the neighborhood. Two typical occupations that dictated that the fathers work different schedules were medical doctors and railroad employees.

Rallings (1966) notes that single men, in larger proportion than single women, had experienced stressful situations in childhood. This finding lends support to the idea that men who remain single are more apt to do so because they are distressed by their early family experience whereas single women do not give evidence of being affected in this way. In addition, more of the single men than the married men in this study exhibited behavior problems as children. The authority system within the family of origin was also associated with subsequent singlehood: Men from democratic families were more likely to marry than were men from authoritarian families. Finally, bachelors were more likely to be the only child or the youngest child with few brothers and sisters. It may be that children from small families learn to be more self-reliant and are more comfortable being on their own. Conversely, these children may miss out on learning skills for relating successfully with others.

PUSHES AND PULLS FOR SINGLES

Although early experiences are important, the factors that socialize us do not end in childhood, or even adolescence. Some of the complex considerations that enter into an adult's decision to choose singlehood as a lifestyle, to live with a lover, to marry, or to separate were presented by Peter Stein (1975, 1978). Just as married individuals give thought to their decision to enter into marriage, remain married, or alter their family makeup by having children, perhaps single individuals examine and re-examine their state even more.

Pressures to evaluate lifestyle are exaggerated for singles because of their status as outsiders or people who are lacking in some way. The questions asked of bachelors include these: "When will you settle down?" "Why can't you get married?" "Don't you want to have children?" "When are you going to grow up and get on with your life?" Stein suggests that "pushes and pulls" toward both marriage and singlehood exist. Pushes represent negative factors in living situations, while pulls represent attractions to a potential new life alteration. These powerful forces have meaning particular to the individual and change for each person over time. The strength of these pushes and pulls also varies according to a number of other variables, including life-cycle stage, sexual identification, extent of involvement with parents and family, availability of friends and peers, and perception of choice.

Pushes into marriage at an early age might come from a desire to leave home, fears of independence, and personal loneliness or isolation. Marriage might also represent a desire for stability during the turbulent changes that take place in a person's early twenties. As a man remains single throughout his twenties and into his thirties, these pushes into marriage probably lose some of their power. For some, dating patterns, parental pressures, a desire for a loving bond with one person and with children, examples from friends, and acceptance of the cultural "script" are pulls toward early involvement and marriage. The positive reasons for single-hood also vary throughout the life cycle. Individuals Stein interviewed who spoke positively about their single status mentioned freedom, career opportunities, friendships, economic self-sufficiency, enjoyable sexual experiences, personal development, and overall life enjoyment as factors in their decision.

The larger society beyond family, friends, and work may also influence one's desire to marry. These cultural conditions change over time. For instance, to be 25 and never-married in 1960 was rare. Beginning about 1979, however, the majority of individuals at age 25 had never been married. These single people are usually drawn to live in cities. "The larger cities of the United States are now sufficiently complex in occupational and social structures to sustain a variety of lifestyles and residential locations with specific lifestyles. . . . Within the heterogeneous areas of the city, singles can share homogeneous areas" (Stein, 1978, p. 6).

Young, urban singles' major concerns are usually with establishing satisfying living arrangements, meeting prospective congenial friends, engaging in activities that they enjoy, and finding meaningful work. Concerns for friendship and social interaction have drawn the attention of the business sector. The result has been profit-making organizations seeking to attract singles. Singles bars and dating services are commercial ventures that come to mind, but also included are less exploitative groups, such as those offering continuing education. Sierra Club newsletters use a bold "S" to designate events that are intended for singles. Tennis clubs sponsor "Meet-A-Partner" nights. Restaurants advertise wine-tasting nights for singles. Singles bars and dating services are not exploitative in and of themselves: Many people see their association with them as uplifting and essential. However, some singles "services" gain much of their attraction by offering to "rescue" singles from their untenable position. Some "entrepreneurs have become skilled in exploiting the needs of single people for self-worth and meaningful relationships through the merchandising of images of glamour and adventure" (Stein, 1975, p. 498). Other non-commercial activities (e.g., church groups, sporting groups, volunteer organizations) continue to meet some of the needs of many urban singles.

As challenging as some of the urban settings may be, rural never-marrieds probably suffer more because resources are even less convenient. Rural people are not as concentrated, so that fewer opportunities are available to meet others and connect with like-minded people. Because this pattern shows no sign of changing, rural single men and women may be forced to choose between their home community and moving to large cities, causing potential estrangement from families.

Finding meaningful work to satisfy economic, psychological, and social needs is not unique to the unmarried. However, work and career may become particularly important to singles. The economic reality of only one potential income source and undivided living expenses may put special demands on them. Work may also be used to provide important psychological benefits. It may be necessary as an avenue to increase self-esteem, to enhance one's sense of mastery and validate one's competence. Employment might also serve to provide a sense of organization, responsibility, and belonging—a way to be connected. Traditional views have proposed that professional employment is essential for the old maid schoolteacher and the workaholic bachelor because they do not have other outlets in which to invest their energy and meet personal needs. Conversely other views hold that singles may be vocationally unreliable because they do not have any responsibilities on the homefront that would keep them tethered to their job. Empirical support for either of these disparate positions does not exist: These observations appear to be part of the overall stereotypical negative view of single adults.

Work may also help singles with the important task of forming social connections with others and developing friendships. In his interviews with unmarried adults Stein consistently found that "the importance of close, caring friendships, based on free choice and developing into a sense of mutuality, were emphasized by single men and women. In their departure from traditional family structures, these single adults express a strong need for substitute networks of human relationships that provide the basic satisfactions of intimacy, sharing and continuity" (Stein, 1981, p. 142). Employment, avocations, hobbies, and other social activities take on additional importance for single people because they increase the opportunity for social networking, which may be more readily available to their married peers.

Throughout history, and still in most societies, friends and friendship needs are met almost exclusively through kinship. This has been seen as the natural and appropriate setting for most interpersonal needs. Friendships outside of the family are often minimized because of their competition with kin. In general, the more traditional the kinship values, the more hostile the views toward outside friendships, which are seen as threatening to the family's sanctity. Because "traditional" individuals may perceive a threat to their family bonds from a single person, singles' efforts to enter into close and intimate relationships can be undermined. Sociologists note that few role models for friendships between married and unmarried friends exist. Instead, friendships between married individuals and their unmarried friends are often viewed with suspicion. Through many overt and covert messages it becomes clear that singles should be friends with other singles. Although this is not an absolute dictum, it makes the period of the twenties a difficult time for singles as their friends get married and their connection with them is seriously strained. And the problem only gets worse through the thirties. As marriages solidify, couples forget what it is like to be single. Having children of their own also further distinguishes married from non-married people.

Non-familial relationships are critical to the development of a successful single life. Studies find that contact with friends and participation in voluntary organizations were better predictors of happiness for the never-married than for the married (Ward, 1979, 1981). But spontaneous gatherings are few for single people: Activities with friends require initiative and planning. This is even more true as the single person ages. As familiarity and ease of availability become more important, networks of friends—a surrogate family that can provide the basic satisfactions of sharing and continuity—often become more elusive. Single people may become despondent or defend against these painful experiences by becoming more self-sufficient: They transcend their longings by becoming self-contained.

Single men can become more isolated in mid-life than unmarried women. Women are usually better socialized for establishing friendships that include the verbal expression of affection: experiencing intimacy, sharing feelings, and carrying on open dialogue are more part of their training than for men. But men do find ways of connecting with one another, often by doing things together. Working to build a tree house or playing on a sports team with its parallel, but shared, activity makes up the foundation for many boys as they learn to be connected. Although the emphasis is more on instrumental activity than the more verbal and relational undertakings of girls, men do learn how to appreciate one another. However, even though these activities can promote relatedness and active interaction with others, males can be limited in the kind and depth of social support they practice. In addition, committed same-sex friendships among men can be made more difficult because of society's homophobic attitudes. For instance, two men going to the movies together can raise eyebrows.

The need for support systems, an important part of personal development in early adulthood, can be even more pronounced as singles move into later life. Retirement can have special impact on never-married adults: It may deprive them of a major source of interpersonal interaction. Psychologist Charles Ward suggests "that single older people have difficulty 'locating' their social personalities since they lack the interpersonal expectations and routines, and associated self-evaluation and self-validation, which arise in a relationship as involved as marriage" (Ward, 1981, p. 354). Even when never-married people have a variety of confidants, they may lack the regular, ready-made availability of those persons when receiving care is necessary. Ward notes that the shrinking life space in old age makes this a critical deficit. Unfortunately the reduced social contacts of later life may increase the need for extended family to provide support at precisely the same time that these supports are less available. Conversely, however, never-married adults may be less prone to the isolation felt by so many older persons as they age. Never-marrieds, Stanley Gubrium determined, have spent a lifetime getting used to being alone. "By old age, these men and women had developed long term strategies for dealing with their state and they did not want to have this social reality disturbed" (Gubrium, 1975, p. 38). In his study, never-married people evaluated everyday life similarly to older married persons in the sense that both are more positive than older divorced or widowed persons. "Compared to other marital statuses, being [never-married] may be a premium in old age in that it avoids the desolation effects of bereavement following spouse death" (Gubrium, 1975, p. 32).

This review of marriage and mental health helps us better understand how these two entities may be related. The larger culture's stereotype and belief that there is something abnormal or peculiar about people who do not marry seem to receive some support from studies reporting that never-married individuals seek more psychological services than do their married counterparts. However, specific, indisputable evidence supporting the overriding public opinion of bachelors as maladjusted and deviant does not exist. More important, these comparisons do not explain what causes the apparent differences in psychological distress: Are they because of different rates of use, psychological distress caused by being single, or singles' predisposition to mental disorder, or is some other factor affecting the results? Although marriage offers many possible positive rewards for people who work to bring them about, marriage can also cause pain and disruption to individuals who have difficulty attaining its benefits.

So the biggest questions still remain: What is at the core of bachelor personality, and how well are bachelors getting along in their lives? The next chapter answers some of these questions by presenting a general overview of the psychological makeup of bachelors. The chapters that follow present specific delineations of the three qualitatively different bachelor personalities.

NOTES

1. A depth review of the hypotheses regarding marriage and the use of mental health services, including studies that support each position, is presented in I. Gotlib and S. McCabe. (1990). Marriage and psychopathology. In F. Fincham & T. Bradbury (Eds.), *The psychology of marriage: Basic issues and applications* (pp. 226–257). New York: Guilford Press.

2. Further support for this position comes from R. Kessler and J. McRae (1984), who observed the sex differences of married and non-married individuals and determined that "[t]he more pronounced sex difference among the married reflects the selection of mentally ill women into marriage and the selection of mentally ill men out of marriage. . . . [T]raditional sex norms make it more difficult for an emotionally disturbed man than an emotionally disturbed woman to marry since the passivity that frequently accompanies mental illness is not so much an impediment to women as to men in the marriage market" (p. 116).

3

THE BACHELOR PERSONALITY: CORE ELEMENTS

Most human behaviors serve a purpose for the person who employs them. Behaviors can be self-protecting or self-promoting. By definition bachelors' behavior includes remaining single by not marrying. In this way they diverge from society's norms. Does the fact that they are atypical with regard to marriage mean that bachelors are weird, aberrant, or abnormal people? In a word the answer is "no." Bachelors as a group are not pathological or disturbed. Bachelors do not have glaring personality exigencies. Nor are they all under five feet tall with adhesive-taped, heavy, black-rimmed eyeglasses and dressed in wrinkled polyester shirts with ink stains in spite of the plastic pocket-protector.

However, bachelors do approach life with certain characteristic patterns and inclinations that make them different from other men. These traits are sometimes subtle and may go unnoticed by people who have only superficial relationships with them. To the persons who strive to be intimately involved with bachelors, however, these attributes become part of their experience with these men. Being too close to a particular bachelor can sometimes muddle the view so that his behaviors are not understood. This chapter steps back from bachelors as individuals in order to examine commonalities and trends in their behaviors and consider what lies under the surface: their traits, defenses, and attitudes.[1]

Describing bachelors with objective distance offers the potential for seeing them clearly. However, the downside of this procedure is that close scrutiny applied to any group usually makes the people being studied look more troubled than they would appear on a day-to-day basis. Most bachelors are competent individuals who are not particularly troubled, but who have made different choices than most men. On the whole they are intelligent. Bachelors often earn advanced degrees and have productive professional careers. There is nothing stopping bachelors from achieving the same personal or financial success as married men. Bachelors are neither loathsome nor despicable. On the contrary, their self-imposed social limitations are rather benign and usually harmless to others. For instance, they do not promise fidelity and then cheat on their wives, marry for money, or abuse their wives. Their "sins" are usually sins of omission. In many ways bachelors, like the rest of us, are getting along in life as best as they can.

For some bachelors being single is an adaptive activity—it is the best choice for them. After all, choosing to not marry does not preclude becoming fully self-actualized, socially productive, and personally satisfied. Although they might be missing out on the productive union possible within a marriage, bachelors sidestep this social activity for which they may be ill-suited. For some bachelors marriage would be an obvious mistake, which would prove traumatic. Marriage would compromise the personal integrity and sense of themselves that many bachelors maintain through their steadfast independent stance. Hopefully no one would advocate that these men marry just to fit in with the majority of Americans because this could be more harmful than helpful to the bachelors—and their wives.

One of the common errors made when scrutinizing bachelors comes from trying to portray them with a single set of descriptors. This homogeneity assumption leads either to watered-down, over-generalized statements or to contradictory descriptors. For instance, general speculations about bachelors range from oversexed playboys to stay-at-home mama's boys: from Captain Kirk to Cliff Claven. Fortunately the reality is far more interesting than assuming that bachelors are all the same. Bachelors have certain common characteristics and attitudes, but the ways bachelors relate to others and their reasons for not marrying can be qualitatively different. These variations in how they get along with others exist along a continuum from the bachelor who has had several multi-year romantic relationships as he negotiated law school and established himself in a corporate setting in which he earns a six-figure salary to the janitor who has never had more than a two-date relationship and has had sex only with prostitutes. Knowing the psychology of bachelors means understanding what they share in common and also appreciating the ways in which they are different.

The core personality traits that bachelors share include

- staunch independence and self-reliance,
- emotional detachment,
- interpersonal passivity, and
- idiosyncratic thinking.

Although these core elements are common to all bachelors,[2] the degree to which they are displayed varies considerably. For some bachelors these traits represent only part of the range of their behaviors. Also, the extent to which they are in conscious awareness (and therefore amenable to change) differs substantially depending on the bachelor. For instance, one man's commitment to independence means that he has never had a woman stay overnight at his apartment, while another man maintains his independence even though he is currently living with a woman. In another example emotional distance is practiced by one bachelor who shares very few of his feelings with his steady girlfriend of two years, while another bachelor's emotional isolation means he has not even considered a romantic relationship for eight years. In these ways the level of comfort and the quality of relationships achieved among bachelors differ markedly.

Differences among bachelors are not random: They follow distinct patterns. Specifically, three bachelor types, based on how uncompromising they are about the core personality elements, exist: *Flexible* bachelors can relax their independent and detached mannerisms to relate positively and successfully, *Entrenched* bachelors cling rigidly and unalterably to autonomy and isolation to protect themselves, and *Conflicted* bachelors are ambivalent and equivocal about how to be independent without feeling detached.

To help the reader follow these differences throughout this book, the Flexible bachelors—the most agile, accomplished, and comfortable men—are all given pseudonyms beginning with the letter "F."

Flexible bachelors will be more fully explored in Chapter 5. Entrenched bachelors, satisfied with their lives because they do not seek deep interactions with others, are all given pseudonyms beginning with the letter "E." Entrenched bachelors will be more fully explored in Chapter 6. In between these two bachelor types are Conflicted and Despondent bachelors, who are ambivalent about interacting with others: They desire independence, but fear isolation; they yearn for others, but get concerned about being dependent. Conflicted and Despondent bachelors are all given pseudonyms beginning with the letter "C" or "D." Conflicted and Despondent bachelors will be more fully explored in Chapter 7. Case studies of each of these bachelor types in their specific chapters will fully explicate what they have in common with other bachelors as well as illustrate how they differ.

The quotations in these chapters are from statements made by the bachelors during personal interviews. They are used to precisely illustrate each individual's experience of the psychological concept being described. Some of these direct quotes are peculiar, as when a bachelor refers to an old girlfriend as "the opposite party" or "the person with whom I spent time." They have not been altered because the stilted communication style, in addition to the idea expressed, says a great deal about the men who made these statements.

INDEPENDENCE AND SELF-RELIANCE

I like being single because if I accomplish something, I feel like I earned it on my own, and it is more satisfying that way. (*Clyde*)

I like to work on my own and call my own shots. Whether I win or lose, I know I did it on my own, for me. (*Elroy*)

Being single, I have a sense of myself by myself, and that is something that married people do not achieve. There is a certain freedom in being able to define myself in myself, free from seeing another person standing next to me when I look in the mirror. (*Doug*)

I have a strong desire for change, and I want to be free to go with the changes. (*Flip*)

One of the paramount core personality traits of bachelors is their allegiance to independence and self-reliance. Bachelors pride themselves on being self-reliant. They highly value their autonomy. The specter of giving up their freedom is not equal to whatever the trade-off might be. Bachelors state that their singleness helps them maintain their personal independence. They value personal freedom so highly that they are afraid marriage would be an intolerable compromise. Even though they are not necessarily doing anything mischievous, they do not want to be accountable to others.

Not being married is one way in which bachelors guard their independence. Remaining single maintains a separateness that works in concert with other overt activities (as well as their inner dynamics) to protect bachelors' high priority on independence. Although their freedom might be considered illusory—after all, anything held too tightly can become restrictive—bachelors organize themselves and their activities around this key element.

Some bachelors are rather matter-of-fact about protecting their liberty through remaining single. For instance, Edgar states, "Men don't get married because they don't want to lose their sense of independence," and Curt thinks that "men just have a sense of not wanting to compromise their time." Some bachelors, however, get distressed discussing what Cliff describes as the "fearsome prospect that marriage will impose demands on my time." Don recognizes that "I'm 44 and I have very strong prejudices about the way I live. I also have a great deal of freedom. It's hard for me to imagine giving those things up."

A high desire for autonomy pervades most bachelors' lives. The detached, reserved, and solitary values that form bachelors' attitudes toward getting married and having a family of their own are not confined to their behavior regarding marriage. Their strong commitment to individualism and self-reliance resonates throughout their undertakings. Bachelors want to do most things on their own. They feel encumbered if they are too involved with other people at work and at home. Earl gives a concrete illustration, to which most people can relate on some level, when he says:

The best thing about being single is that I know where the TV remote is. I love that. But, even more important, if I don't know where it is, I know that I am responsible for it not being there. No one else can get in and muck up my life. I don't have to ask someone else where it is if I can't find it. I have gotten very used to having this kind of organization and control, and I don't think I want to give it up.

Where other people are likely to see socializing as an opportunity for positive involvement, bachelors are more likely to see fraternizing as an obstacle. Drake relates, "Having a girlfriend has many advantages, don't get me wrong, but it also means that I give up a lot of my freedom, and that I cannot stand." Bachelors avoid interdependence. Compromising their individualism is onerous. A typical example is Carl, who states that when dating

> I did not enjoy, at times, being depended upon. I like being around someone, but I did not like having her want me to be a certain way for her. On the other hand there are just as many times that I might not have enjoyed being depended upon as the opposite party did not enjoy me depending upon them. It is very hard to strike a balance. Being depended upon can bring heavy pressure.

Like many bachelors Carl does not appreciate that intimate relationships can be mutual and reciprocal—instead, he feels a girlfriend is a burden. Perhaps this is because bringing about mutuality in a relationship would be improbable for him. His high commitment to independence forecloses mutuality as an option. His commitment to self-determination makes it unlikely that he will be able to achieve the interdependent reliance that makes marriage worthwhile.

Flip's decision to stay single is connected to his desire to avoid relying on other people to run his restaurant. "If I had a wife and family, I would have to give up the hands-on operation of my business." Doug likes having "total freedom of movement. I can decide how and what I want to do and just do it. I mean, that does get old sometimes, but it is nice to have when I want it." Cliff sees his world similarly as he states, "If I want to go to the Bahamas for a weekend, I can just decide to do it, pick up, and go. I don't have to check with anyone."

Bachelors prefer not having to negotiate and possibly compromise. Earl relates, "I just don't have to confer with anyone else, and I like that." Along these lines Foster relates that "I like to know what my plans are for the week, and I don't want to have them changed by someone else." Eric says, "I have to have my alone time, I need this because I am basically a loner, and I might not get this if I was married." Similarly Forest states, "Because I am single, I can get my solitude when I want it, no questions asked." A hint of underlying insecurity (common to Conflicted bachelors) comes out as Curt states how important his independence is to him: "I have the freedom to make my own decisions without consultation, and I have the freedom to make my own mistakes without having to worry about whether there are consequences on other people."

Because bachelors value their autonomy, they are reluctant to affiliate. They are careful not to place their welfare in the hands of others. Bachelors clearly like not having to be accountable to someone else, and they see this as a real advantage of being single. Bachelors are used to a life in which they determine their own comings and goings, and they are reluctant to relinquish what they consider to be a preeminent benefit of being single.

The sacrifice of individual freedom for the good of the couple threatens the personal integrity of some bachelors. They would have a difficult time feeling good about themselves if they were married. For all people interpersonal relationships are characterized by maintaining a balance among what is good for *me*, what is good for *you*, and what is good for *us*. Maintaining individuality while also engaging empathically in a positive partnership is always a challenge. Everyone copes and adapts to these different demands with their own personal styles and patterns.

Many people are well suited for the flexibility and compromise that make for a strong marriage. Others exchange their wedding vows and take on the pretenses of being married, but never really enter into a psychological union with their spouse. They remain independent out of a misunderstanding of what it means to be a fully functioning couple, a general indifference to sharing further with their partner, or an anxious withdrawal from the challenges that are involved when interacting with someone else. Intimate involvement with another person offers wonderful possibilities and potentials, but can also be threatening. Never-married men foreclose the potential riches of marriage because avoiding the possible hardship seems safer than accepting the possible loss of individuality that comes with marriage. Bachelors may have some compatriots (currently or formerly married) who would support and affirm their position, but their happily married brothers would tell them that taking the risk is well worth it.

Self-determination seems to be a non-negotiable value that keeps bachelors going. But a lot of men and women feel that independence is important, and they still become happily married. What else is it about bachelors that makes them remain single in order to maintain their independence? The answer lies in their styles of relating, their psychological ego defenses.

EGO DEFENSES

Ego defense is a term first used by Sigmund Freud to describe automatic, unconscious strategies performed by one's rational mind to reduce the anxiety surrounding uncomfortable experiences.[3] Ego defenses describe the styles that people use to relate to their world. A variety of defense mechanisms reduces or conceals the threats a person feels. The primary defense mechanism is repression, in which unacceptable or unpleasant emotions are pushed out of consciousness. Ego defenses serve the important function of helping people modulate and deal with stimulation. They help us cope. While everyone uses ego defenses to get along in the world, some people are more aware of them than others, and some ego defenses are more adaptive than others.

Such defenses can be problematic when a person has a limited assortment of ways to manage conflicts and assuage anxiety. A person who shows a greater variety of defenses with which to manage stressful situations is more likely to deal resourcefully and effectively with problems. Defense mechanisms can also be pathological when only primitive and less mature defenses get enacted. Projection, for instance, in which a person attributes his or her own feelings to someone else, is a relatively immature defense when compared to a defense such as sublimation, in which a person diverts unwanted impulses into socially acceptable thoughts, feelings, or behaviors. Immature defenses are identifiable by the degree to which they distort reality and therefore impede one in dealing accurately and effectively with the real source of the problem. Ego defenses that are enacted with a total lack of awareness or control by the person pose another potential harm. The ability to reflect on and consciously appraise the operation of one's automatic reactions can lead to more direct and constructive problem resolution.

Three primary defenses—emotional detachment, interpersonal passivity, and idiosyncratic thinking—are common among never-married men. These defenses are not among the most mature and adaptive that most adults practice. Although these mechanisms are consistently seen among bachelors, the degree of implementation, their influence on relating, and the degree to which they are under conscious control vary greatly according to the three bachelor types. Because of this, the degree to which they impair each bachelor's ability to achieve mature mutuality in his interpersonal relationships also varies.

EMOTIONAL DETACHMENT

Maybe I just haven't ever loved anyone; maybe that is why I am not married. (*Ethan*)

Sure, I've considered marriage, but there is so much to think about, so much involved, that I never gave it much thought. (*Floyd*)

I considered marrying Mary, but after a while it seemed like we were not on the same page, so we drifted apart. When she left, that was okay with me. (*Felix*)

Bachelors are emotionally guarded people. They are unlikely to have rich and vivid emotional lives. At times they may seem like they have no feelings, or that they are detached from their feelings. Emotional detachment, or isolation of affect, in which people block their feelings and react to events without emotions, is a primary defense mechanism practiced by never-married men. Relating to their worlds with muted feelings is a pervasive characteristic of bachelors' lives.

The limitations of their emotions are seen in both the amount and the range of feelings they have: In most areas of their lives emotions are cut off and repressed. Although it is difficult to describe something that is not there, like emotional responsiveness, there are many telltale signs of emotional detachment among bachelors. For instance, bachelors are more likely to talk about what they *think* about something than how they *feel* about it. Also evident among bachelors are muted emotional words: They *like* rather than *love* someone; they *kind of enjoy* their hobbies rather than *savoring* them; they say that a vacation was *okay* rather than *great*. Emotional detachment was also clearly evident in the way they responded to the Rorschach task. They were more likely to respond to the shape of the blot rather than the color or shading features, a signal that they keep their emotions at bay. They also gave fewer than expected responses to the cards with vivid colors on them, another indicator of emotional withdrawal.

While this emotional constriction may help them manage situations that they would find stressful, it also leads to disinterest. At times bachelors appear estranged or indifferent because they are distant from their feelings. Compared to other men, bachelors are more likely to solve problems dispassionately. Dylan displays this style of relating when describing a conversation with his last girlfriend: "Honest to God, she kept asking about how I felt about her, and I just couldn't think at all what she meant. I told her that I really didn't have any feelings about her staying or going, which just got her very angry." Frank shows his ability to distance himself from feelings when he relates that he feels "very lucky . . . [that I didn't marry an old girlfriend] because she has severe, severe leukemia . . . with the health problems, she's miserable company." Chris relates that "I went out with a few great women during my twenties and thirties, but once we decided to not see each other anymore, I couldn't care at all about them and couldn't get rid of them fast enough."

By isolating feelings, some bachelors interact with others with indifference and estrangement. Through emotional detachment bachelors view broken relationships dispassionately, with an aloof and cavalier sense. Because feelings are repressed, bachelors can interact with others on a superficial level, and this maintains their independence because they do not become emotionally involved with others. Bachelors remain peripheral to deeply intimate relationships because they limit the depth of emotionality that they experience.

INTERPERSONAL PASSIVITY

When I was dating Alice, she used to ask me what I wanted to do. However, I usually kept what I wanted to do to myself and tried to second-guess what she wanted to do. Then we'd do what she wanted to do, and it wasn't much fun for me. (*Dick*)

I'm not very good at saying what I want from other people, so I like to keep to myself. (*Ethan*)

Most bachelors tend to be passive and unassertive. Although many confidently apply themselves in their careers, they tend to be tentative when approaching others. This observation comes as a major blow to those stereotypes that maintain that bachelors are the swingingest of singles. Unassertiveness is part of a package wherein bachelors withdraw from others by being, as they say, "very shy" or "overly cautious." Other bachelors say they do not get what they want when interacting with others because they are "very easygoing" or "really laid back." Their difficulty with asserting themselves makes bachelors hesitant to get involved with others because their autonomy is threatened. Shortcomings in maintaining their own positions when negotiating both mundane and important aspects of relationships make them want to keep to themselves. For instance, Don laments that "I simply don't have enough money to ask a woman out," but he does not ask for a raise or look for a new job. Clive is not sure that the classes he is taking will count toward the graduate degree he desires, but he does not ask a school administrator who could give him an answer.

Passivity is a psychological trait that can be seen behaviorally as avoidance—steering clear of obstacles in one's path. Avoidance among never-married men is observed in both obvious and subtle ways. The Rorschach test with bachelors showed a subtle avoidance of the task. The most obvious technique of limiting the number of responses was utilized by only a few individuals. However, avoidance through restraint and withdrawal was highly evident. Bachelors answered with an overabundance of responses that referred to the shape of the inkblots, while dismissing or neglecting potentially complex and creative aspects of the task. They made greater use of simple and economical responses that ignored many factors. They tended to overlook details. By ignoring details, avoiding the complexity of a situation, and responding with a sense of formality, they made simple and "safe" responses. Not incorporating details means that while bachelors formulate solutions apparently adequate to the challenge, their interactions are constricted and cautious. Repetitiveness is another strategy used by some bachelors. In all these ways a subtle form of non-participation or rejection of the Rorschach task was utilized.

Interpersonally, avoidance manifests itself in the complacency and lack of engagement with which many bachelors approach other people. The bachelors who fear they lack proficiency in getting what they need when interacting with others withdraw from intimate relations in order to maintain their independence. David illustrates this process when he reflects on a past relationship and says, "It always felt like we did what she wanted to do. And maybe that was because I didn't usually have a lot of suggestions about what to do, but I got tired of her setting the agenda, so I just stopped talking with her."

PASSIVITY IN SEXUALITY

Many people shy away from meaningful encounters because they feel unable to hold their own when negotiating. This seems especially true for bachelors. When talking about his restricted sexual involvement with old girlfriends, Curt offered a superb analogy for how he protects himself by limiting his involvements. A chef himself, Curt elaborated as follows:

> A restaurant, you see, has a certain ethos and character, and it must have the right people, or it cannot be itself; it will have to change. Certain people who know how to use it are necessary for the restaurant to keep its character. For instance, if a restaurant goes from being a casual diner to becoming a businessman's restaurant, it must change. Some restaurant managers will screen out business-men, or otherwise they will turn into a different kind of place. Or they say it about tourists. At times they could fill the place with tourists, but then it would become a different kind of place, so they try to keep the number of casual customers down to a minimum so that they don't take over the character of the place. Or a play for that matter. Not only does it need an audience, but the right kind, the kind that permits it to be what it is. And that is certainly true of people.

Like his example, Curt has maintained his own character by controlling his "clientele": He has had only one adult sexual rela-tionship. He explains that "my temperament generally doesn't meld well in that way."

Bachelors are reticent and reluctant to get involved, to make demands, or to assert their needs in the important areas of sexual expression and friendships. Again contrary to some stereotypes bachelors tend to be passive and hesitant in expressing their sexuality. For instance, Erwin relates, "I was always interested in sex, but it was difficult to know how to read my girlfriends. Did she want to fool around? I could never get around to asking this question or initiate much activity, so it wasn't until my late twenties that I first had sex. And even since then it hasn't been too often."

Among the bachelors interviewed the average age of first sexual intercourse was 23 years. Although comparative numbers are hard to come by, almost two-thirds of the bachelors felt that their own sexual development was later than that of their peers. Dick, who had his first intercourse at age 30 with the woman who remains his only sexual partner, shows his reticence in sexual relationships, as he speculates:

> Like most high school kids I thought about sex a lot, but I would never have had a sexual relationship in high school for fear, "What if I get her pregnant?" or "What if she thinks I love her when all I was was horny at the time?" . . . So I didn't, and I wouldn't do it in college even though certainly the thought occurred to me 'cause I thought, "Gee, this is a small college. If this ever got around this campus, I'd be a marked man," because they were so conservative. So I was very particular not to have a sexual relationship with these women although certainly I would have liked to, but I thought I'd be getting in over my head.

Derrick, too, was afraid of being overly active in initiating sexual involvement:

> The first woman that I dated, I thought I was going to marry, but I never had sexual relations with her. You know, we necked a lot and that sort of thing. At that time she was a Catholic, but she didn't want to permit intercourse, and I didn't want to force myself on her. . . . It was later on, I was about 28 or 29, when I first started having sex. And that was as much her decision as it was mine.

Duane, a quiet, unassuming bachelor, states:

> Some of my girlfriends have wanted sex and some haven't. But, as I say, I'm not an aggressive person, so I don't kind of initiate this. I sort of wait for the signals to arise, and if they do, fine, then I'm lucky, but if not, okay, they don't. I never force myself on a person. I don't think that is appropriate. That's something I would feel very bad about doing.

Duane missed the point that there is intermediate ground between passively awaiting signals and using force. Many people know how to give signals or request them directly.

Passivity, and the lack of assertiveness, in sexual expression, friendships, and significant relationships manages bachelors' potential risk. Steering clear of intimate interactions and minimizing investment in others protect bachelors' personal autonomy and integrity. Passivity in sexual experiences most certainly changed the life histories for some bachelors compared to their married cohort. That is, some men in this age group married because their sexual activity led to pregnancy and they "had to" get married. Men who were not having sex, bachelors included, avoided this possibility.

Almost half of the bachelors interviewed reported that "almost all" of their serious relationships in adulthood have involved sexual intercourse. However, about half of them were inconsistent in this regard: intercourse was not part of the sexual expression in many of their relationships. Age and prior sexual experience were two influences in determining whether or not relationships tended to include intercourse, but several men's experiences have involved a mixture of "serious" relationships that "went all the way" and those that did not. A relatively passive stance appeared to be present within their sexual relationships, as reflected in this mixture of coital and non-coital relations. For instance, when asked "Have all your serious relationships involved sexual relations?" Fred responds, "All but one [relationship] did, and that was her choice; she didn't want to have sex, and I didn't want to push her." Frank is more calculating as he answers the question by saying, "The answer to the question is 'No,' they did not all involve sexual relations. But some of them were just because I wasn't there yet. Some relationships that happened a little later in life may not have involved sex, but that wasn't for lack of hope on my part."

By and large the men interviewed were hesitant when talking about their sexual relations. In interviews this took the form of mild anxiety and annoyance, manifested in quick and perfunctory responses that lacked elaboration. Several men actively avoided questions of sexuality. This does not seem so unusual given the age and gender of the individuals involved. However, it also seems to reflect the way these men would act with their partners. The result is that some bachelors look like passive onlookers to their own lives. For instance, Dick, reaching a growing sense of stagnation and boredom with his weekly Saturday night sex with his girlfriend, bought a copy of the *The Joy of Sex*, but did nothing but put it on her nightstand hoping that she would get the point. Another onlooker, Earl, who has been dating the same woman for 18 years, states that although he does not really like it, he has accepted that his girlfriend decided three years ago that they should not have sexual relations, so they do not.

Lack of sexual assertiveness is also reflected in their low participation in sexual relations: One-quarter of the bachelors interviewed reported two or fewer sexual partners throughout adulthood, and another third reported between three and six partners. Although this might not be far from the norm, it certainly contrasts with the Don Juan bachelor stereotype.

PASSIVITY IN FRIENDSHIPS

Friendships comprise another area in which bachelors' passivity limits their interactions. The idea of friends and friendships, male and female, is of interest to most bachelors, certainly to the Flexible and Conflicted ones. Flip relates that "having friends is very important to me," and Dick is similarly appreciative of their value as he says, "My friends are among the most important things I have." However, bachelors do not usually put great energy into friendships, and elaborate comments about friendships rarely come up during interviews. Bachelors talk about friendships in a brief, cursory manner. When they are delved into, friendships are usually spoken of in terms of something missing in a bachelor's life.

At the same time almost all bachelors have at least a couple of men they call friends. Consistent with most men, friendships are based more on mutual activities than on shared emotions. For instance, playing sports together or belonging to a similar group activity was instrumental in bringing these bachelors together with others. Fewer, though some, men spoke about the close and intimate interactions that they found in their friendships.

Very few bachelors are disinterested in friendships. Most bachelors value friendships and wish to increase this aspect of their lives. However, they rarely take direct steps to try to bring this about. In addition, having friends is not so easy. Some of the difficulties in having male companions come from the sense of competitiveness that emerges among men. For instance, Dean relates that "having guy friends is not very satisfying because they are so competitive."

The differences in being single with married friends and the time demands that having a family puts on a bachelor's married friends are also reported as problems for bachelors trying to connect with others. Their reserve in not making friends may also be influenced by the fact that part of what is valued in important friends is sharing an established history. Like many people, bachelors' best friends are the ones that go back to college days or other earlier times when they shared important life circumstances. As bachelors lament not seeing their friends as much as they used to, there is a sense of melancholy. For instance, Floyd relates, "This is the biggest lack in my life right now, not having two or three good male friends in Chicago. I have lots of male friends in New York City, mostly old college friends, but I miss having guys to just call for tennis and dinner and talk."

Bachelors are mixed on whether it is easier to be friends with a woman than a man. Women can be difficult to be friends with because they sometimes share fewer common interests and because there is the potential to be misunderstood as a sexual partner. But most bachelors say they value and maintain women friends. At the same time the distinction between friendship and romantic involvement poses problems for many of them, particularly for Conflicted bachelors. For instance, Don disgustedly states:

> I'd like to have women friends, but I don't really feel that you can have women friends. It's like I've never met a woman yet who wants to be friends. They say friendship, but what they actually mean is they want you to date them, take them out and foot the bill. If they feel you have prospects, they will continue with you; otherwise, they just don't call.

Doug is more generous as he strives to "distinguish less sharply between women friends and women 'special-relationships.' I'm trying to smudge those borders between the special, exclusive relationship and the category of friend. I would like to bring those two together and have easier, more comfortable times with women."

Clarifying the distinction between friendships and romance is also a concern of Dick's as he relates, "There are some women at church who I consider friends, women who call and I talk with them on the phone, but I don't spend time with them. I would like to. I think part of the problem is that if she's being friendly to me,

I don't know from my perception if she's coming on to me or if she's just being friendly." Dennis also appears confused about mixed roles as he relates, "There is a woman living downstairs from me I would just as soon have been friends with. I mean, that's what I tried to do with her, become basically a friend. But it's turned into a sexual thing, and she wants it a great deal, so she shows all sort of unsatisfaction that I won't look at her romantically."

Perhaps because of these confusing dilemmas, friendships with women appear to lack spontaneity—they are usually preplanned. For instance, Doug says that he "plays weekly tennis with a woman friend," and Forest has a woman friend "with whom I have dinner every Monday and we shoot the breeze."

In promoting sexuality and friendship bachelors are apprehensive about the price they might pay if they assert themselves. If they are assertive with others, bachelors would feel responsible for the outcome. Therefore, they back away from being assertive. Detachment from personal responsibility for a particular situation because you do not initiate the behavior is made possible by personal passivity and tolerance in letting other people make decisions.

Passivity is observable in bachelors' overt statements as well as in the style and tone of their presentations. Bachelors frequently pepper their conversations with phrases like "I don't really care about that," "it was really up to her," "I never really thought about that," and "who's to know?" At other times they talk about "wishing" or "hoping" that certain life events were different, while not seizing their role in bringing about their goals. Many bachelors appear to react instinctively with privacy, reticence, and hesitance both interpersonally and professionally.

One result of their passivity is that some bachelors appear to drift into permanent single status rather inadvertently. No bachelor interviewed had made up his mind early on in his teens or twenties that he would be a bachelor. They simply develop patterns of low interaction with others, and because of the comfort that freedom brings them, they choose the path of least resistance. Bachelors tend to not be risk takers, but instead simply continue familiar behavior. As they float down their own river of life, they are carried along submissively by the currents that prevail. In addition, unlike some of their married peers, bachelors seem to drift along with their arms tightly wrapped around themselves so that they have fewer contacts with others. Their personal choices are made by inactivity: Opportunities not taken become choices made. Many bachelors appear to just go along for the ride without clearly defining their values or asserting a personal position.

IDIOSYNCRATIC THINKING

Idiosyncratic thinking, seeing things in novel ways different from one's peers, is the third major defense mechanism used often by bachelors. The distorted thinking in the bachelor's mechanism makes stressful situations more manageable by contorting them so they can be interpreted from a uniquely personal vantage point, which makes sense to him. In the general population distortion ranges from psychotic activity like hallucinations or delusions to the more common practice of seeing things idiosyncratically—how we would like them to be. On a day-to-day basis bachelors show more of the latter distortion—applying their own unique meaning to ambiguous events. The result is that their perceptions are often inconsistent with what most people might see and report. The process of reshaping a challenge to suit inner needs can be adaptive some of the time: Idiosyncratic thinking can lead to unique solutions to problems or to creative divergences from traditional thinking. However, getting along with others is difficult when people are buying into different basic assumptions about the world.

Distortions among never-married men mostly arise from vague or inarticulate communication or from behavioral miscues, which interfere with their ability to get along with others in work and in love. Ethan thinks his boss is petty and closed-minded just because he expects his workers to show up before the shop opens. Eric shows some poor judgment in bringing an umbrella with him to his interview on an absolutely clear day. Cliff offers his interviewer a beer at the beginning of his 10:00 A.M. interview. Craig responds that four of the ten Rorschach cards look like vaginas (it is rare to report even one). Although these miscalculations are not in and of themselves disturbed, they mark each of these men as being somewhat out of step with others.

Interviews give some indications of distortion. For instance, the fact that almost all bachelors expect that they probably will marry is quite improbable. While it is possible for a man to marry at any age, the odds decrease dramatically over time: 20 to 1 against for a never-married man who is 45 years old. The likelihood of marriage is even more unlikely because many bachelors interviewed were not currently involved in relationships, nor did they have any real prospects. But interviews elicit self-descriptions, necessarily subjective and uncorroborated. Therefore, distortions are difficult to detect in this material. Idiosyncratic thinking, however, was clearly evident in the Rorschach study conducted. In general, the bachelors tended to be unusual in the way they look at circumstances and describe events. They do not intend to actively deceive others, but particularly in unstructured situations bachelors tend to be unorthodox in their perceptions. They are likely to give novel, atypical, low-frequency responses.

Another example of extremely distorted thinking was Ernie's report that coworkers at three different jobs "tried to poison me because I was the new guy and they wanted to keep their group the way it was." Eric's experience is more typical of bachelors when he relates that "I don't understand people well. Sometimes when I am in a room with others and they are talking about something, I can't even begin to see it the same way they do, so I just shut up and keep to myself."

Chet's assertion that "I would have married her, but we lived in different towns" is an example of another common distortion seen in bachelors. They sometimes implicate external sources—fate or life circumstances—rather than recognizing their own responsibility. When other factors are seen as responsible for activity, people can wash their hands of accountability. Putting the responsibility on others also reduces the level of investment in the outcome and avoids potential problems by minimizing feelings about events.

Some bachelors also use an amorphous style of communication that is characterized by a tendency to miss or blur differences and to overlook details. Because of this, they can homogenize the varied elements of their background, making it difficult to know what their experience is. This also makes it hard for some bachelors to know what is going on with others. Elmo, for instance, states, "When my girlfriend left with that other guy, I had no sense that anything was wrong, and I was shocked." Clyde similarly seems confused about himself and others as he states, "I'd like to be able to make friends with people easier. That, I think, would be useful to say the least. I mean 'useful,' but I don't know how I'd define it."

Living alone, as most bachelors do, and therefore having no need to clarify information to conform to the perceptions of a partner, may allow their minor distortions to continue without modification. People living on their own can cling to personal beliefs without concern about consensual validation: Believing that it is not unusual to live in an apartment for seven years without putting up any pictures, as Edgar did, can be viewed as normal if no one comes to visit. Although distortion can be socially disruptive, bachelors perform with an adequate level of reality testing when confronted with structured tasks and demands. In addition, bachelors' misinterpretations of common situations are amenable to correction. Bachelors do not have the fixed false beliefs seen in delusional people. But bachelors tend to be inarticulate when talking about others, which makes reciprocal friendships and love relationships difficult. They are not tied to conventional standards.

SUMMARY OF CORE PERSONALITY ELEMENTS

These three defensive maneuvers—emotional detachment, interpersonal passivity, and idiosyncratic thinking—ward off uncomfortable feelings and anxieties for bachelors. These defenses also contribute to and work in concert with their high desire for independence and their desire to be self-reliant. The independence that they so highly value is vigorously upheld by these unconscious maneuvers: Emotionally detached people are less likely to enter into mutually beneficial relationships, passive men avoid linking up with others, and seeing the world idiosyncratically makes independence all the more necessary. Conversely, their independence allows these particular defenses to go unchallenged. Although these core personality elements undergird the bachelor personality, the degree to which bachelors are bound to them varies greatly. Even so, each of these four core elements of the bachelor personality has a critical role in determining their actions and attitudes regarding marriage.

NOTES

1. The bachelor personality described here derives from three sources. First, prior scientific studies about never-married men were reviewed and compiled—many of these were covered briefly in Chapter

2. Second, depth interviews were conducted with bachelors about their personal undertakings. Third, Rorschach inkblot tests were administered to a sample of bachelors. The complete Rorschach study underlying this work is published in C. A. Waehler. (1991). Selected Rorschach variables of never-married men. *Journal of Clinical Psychology, 47,* 123–132. Copies of this study are available from the author.

2. Obviously not all bachelors will fit the parameters of this review; human nature is too complex for that. As with any population, some bachelors are unique in the way they go about their lives, so these men defy categorization. Other men lie outside the "norms" established in this material simply because the focus here is on describing men in the mainstream of American life. In addition, examinations of bachelors in this study have focused exclusively on Caucasians. Men living far from the average lifestyle (e.g., Hollywood stars or other wealthy men) have different cultural demands placed on them and are least likely to fit the bachelor types explored in this book.

3. A terrific introduction to Freud's thinking is presented in a series of dynamic lectures he delivered during his only trip to the United States. These lectures are compiled in S. Freud, (1909). *Five lectures on psycho-analysis* (J. Strachey, trans.). New York: Norton.

4

BACHELOR VIEWS OF MARRIAGE

Marriage isn't a bad thing, but it really is simply used as a social rite of passage. Men get married because they are expected to; it is a convention. They do it from habit because nothing else occurs to them. They probably get something from it, but it is also a desire to preserve and perpetuate the past. It also serves as a protection, to make a person more acceptable. (*Curt, who believes he will one day be married*)

Part of what we see in bachelors' views of marriage is that they are not so different from other people. Like most people, bachelors appropriately view marriage cautiously. This stance appreciates the challenges entailed in this serious, lifelong commitment. By contrast a "Prince Charming and Cinderella living happily ever after" attitude would be naive and ill-advised. When considering the question "Is marriage good?" the answer must begin as so many in psychology do: "It depends. . . . " Marriage in and of itself is not necessarily positive or negative. Certainly the potential benefits reviewed in Chapter 2 are tremendous. But bachelors tend to be more in touch with marriage's potential drawbacks. They seem keenly aware that some people lose a lot more than they gain in marriage. To some degree marital fortune depends on conditions that impact the couple. However, whether a marriage is ultimately successful or not depends primarily on the constructive efforts of each partner and the relationship they are able to create for themselves. What we can see by examining bachelors' views of marriage is how the core elements of their personalities—uncompromising independence, emotional detachment, interpersonal passivity, and idiosyncratic thinking—play out as they consider their serious relationships.

Although it goes against the grain of most of society, not marrying ought to remain a viable and legitimate option free from social reprobation. By making marriage optional, we actually increase its integrity as an institution to be taken seriously. Marriage is not something to be treated lightly or to be engaged in by every person regardless of his or her personal disposition. Marriage is an enterprise that is not right for everyone, nor is everyone well suited for marriage. Not marrying is a logical, optimal choice for some people. And single people should not be penalized for their choice simply because they take an option few others do.

Contrary to some stereotypes most bachelors do not hold marriage in contempt. Neither do they play it up as something they really cannot live without. When asked, most bachelors express a positive view of marriage in general. Bachelors are not so out of the mainstream of society that they do not see the potential value of marriage. In their restrained way they recognize that marriage has advantages that, if achieved, can bring positive benefits. Most bachelors have seriously considered marriage for themselves at some time in their lives.

Further bolstering the concept of idiosyncratic thinking, which sometimes distorts perceptions, is the astonishing observation that most bachelors expect to some day be married. This prediction runs counter to statistical predictions. Another way it shows some unclear thinking is that bachelors are unlikely to marry because many are not seeking spouses, nor are some of them even dating. So just what is going on with these men? In many ways bachelors are the kind of people who wade tentatively into the shallow end of a swimming pool: When they say they probably will marry, they are getting a little wet, but nobody is jumping in. Sometimes marriage requires a big leap. Second, although they do not have anything against marriage, bachelors derive many benefits from not being married. About half of the bachelors interviewed feel whole, complete, and satisfied without being married. These men lack the incentive to take the plunge. The other half recognize genuine drawbacks to remaining single, but their personality style and ambivalent feelings keep them from diving in.

Some bachelors are single only because the women they asked to marry them said no. Earl, for instance, has always intended to marry, but has not "because she didn't say yes." A respected podiatrist who is the junior partner in a three-office practice, Earl has been in a position to marry. He asked Brenda, his girlfriend of 18 years, to marry him in both the third and the twelfth years of their relationship. He rationalizes her refusals by saying, "She has a hard time making decisions and doesn't think I'm the best person she can find. Maybe she is looking for someone more intelligent and more financially successful." Earl cannot have a very good opinion of himself if he has been carrying around this idea that the woman he loves has been looking over his shoulder for someone better than him for 15 years. Or maybe he is just not clear about Brenda's reasoning. In either case, his personal passivity keeps him from moving on to someone else.

Earl is not the only bachelor who had his proposal turned down, yet does not fault the woman for her decision. For example, Clive is disappointed that, as he has convinced himself, his proposal was turned down because he did not make enough money. Ernie, who is more indifferent to marriage, says, "I think I gave her the idea that I wouldn't work on being a good husband, so that is why I am not married. And there might be some truth to that."

Some other bachelors attribute some external third factor as being responsible for their remaining single. Craig states, "Luck just wasn't on my side, so we drifted apart," and Felix conveys, "The timing was always wrong. I was in school or she was busy traveling for her job." Flip unemotionally observes, "I went away for graduate school and the distance took its toll." What can be seen in these men's statements is their passive restraint. They have been emotionally distant and interpersonally passive, so that marriage has been passed up rather than being sought after. Perhaps these men are the male equivalents of Snow White, who waits passively asleep for her prince to rescue her into marriage. This attitude is counterproductive for both genders, but is probably more problematic for men, since it goes against traditional sex-role stereotypes, wherein the men are supposed to be more assertive. And in some ways their personality characteristics may have served them well in not leading to promises that they would later not want to honor.

Some of their divorced cohort may have wished they had shown similar hesitance about getting married.

EMOTIONALLY DETACHED

Consistent with their emotional detachment, bachelors do not tend to use highly emotional words to describe marriage. Only a few bachelors give lip service to the notion that people get married for emotional comfort and companionship. Bachelors are more likely to mention society's expectations as a prime reason men get married. As Eric says, "Men are supposed to marry, everyone knows that this is traditionally part of growing up." The emotional virtues of marriage are most likely to be mentioned by Flexible bachelors. For instance, Forest acknowledges the powerful bond possible in marriage as he states, "Men get married because they love someone and they want a life together with another person. They find someone with whom they can be cooperative, and together they do positive things, like have children." Felix also recognizes the emotional aspects of marriage by explaining his belief that "people find marriage psychologically comforting. They gain an emotional security."

But many bachelors reduce marriage to a social obligation. As Edgar puts it, "Marriage is a social ritual people go through to be considered normal and healthy." This perspective is part of bachelors' reduced emotional lives: Their general pattern is to approach most of life without investing it with lots of feelings. They view marriage dispassionately; marriage is a functional activity serving the participants and society. A few bachelors are cynical in this regard, as when Ernest comments that "there is a certain stabilizing force for our country when most people are getting married; that is why people do it."

But most bachelors are simply nonplussed about marriage. Exemplifying the emotionally flat bachelor, Duane states, "Men get married just because it is time to do so." Similarly Ethan says, "Guys [marry] just because it is time to settle down." Chris agrees that "a guy marries because he just gets tired of the rat race." Bachelors who view marriage as a functional enterprise and remove the emotional aspects that are so much a part of it, are less inclined to see the benefits of companionship.

Some focus on marriage as a method for overcoming personal deficiencies. Along these lines Doug says, "Marriage fulfills a need to be tied to someone, so that the need to have someone else around to do things for them is met. They need to be symbiotically tied . . . lots of people have a need to connect." Clive observes:

My brother really had to get married. Not because she was pregnant, but because he didn't have the ability to take care of himself on his own. He had no social graces and no clue about the basics of how to take care of himself, so I think he saw the easiest solution was to find someone who could give him these things. And he did, and it worked out reasonably well, for him, anyway.

What seems to be missing in these observations is the potential growth and change that come from joining with another person. More than just "adding on a partner" who can make up for personal shortcomings, marriage and close associations can transform people, so that they become more capable, competent, and interesting.

Some bachelors are annoyed by social expectations that men must marry; they resent feeling like less of a person because they are single. A minority of bachelors voice this position vehemently, while others are less direct in their antipathy. Statements reflecting these feelings include Eddie's comment that people "marry for social reasons, to be a regular person," and Dick's observation that "there is a certain status achieved by being married." Doug seems to imply that marriage is a necessary nuisance as he says, "Men get married because they come to a point where they don't know what else to do with their lives." Felix observes, "If a person is not married by age 30, he is suspect, not normal, out of sync with the normal rhythms of life."

But not all bachelors are cynical about marriage's role in society. Some are simply indifferent to marriage, like Fred, who states, "I never had any real desire to do something about getting married." Although he has been engaged twice, Flip says, "I just haven't wanted to get married; I just haven't cared about it," and thus he has not followed through with his two engagements.

Some bachelors simply have little desire to marry. In this vein, and exemplifying the indifference with which he goes about most of his life, Elmo states, "It is just that marriage has never occurred to me." Felix similarly observes, "Marriage is something I just haven't thought about. I guess I never had any real drive to get married. I am glad I'm not married. Often talking about getting married has been the reason why my relationships broke up: She wanted to talk about it, and I could care less." "Why bother with formality?" asks Eddie, who has lived with a serious lover. Felix, a college professor who had dated a few of his former students, gives several reasons why he has not married: "Sometimes they didn't want to marry me; sometimes I didn't want to marry that particular person. Stickier were matters of age differences and different life agendas. Marriage creates more problems than it solves."

These statements seem cold, and they are. The lack of feelings in their observations makes marriage into a thinking activity. At least 25 percent of bachelors, the Entrenched bachelors, appear to be quite indifferent to interpersonal relationships in general and marriage in particular. "Some men just don't care to get married" is a common response during interviews with these men. Ernie is really talking about himself when he suggests that "bachelors just don't have the same needs as other people." Eric offers another benign observation that bachelors "just don't care about marriage, they have nothing against it and nothing for it."

However, other men who initially appear to view marriage dispassionately have an undertone of rancor about it. For instance, Chris relates, "Some people don't need marriage. They are kind of asexual, and they think that women are not worth the bullshit." Similarly Evan states that bachelors "may feel women aren't worth the effort." Another negative statement is made by Duane, who reveals his usually well-guarded low self-opinion as he relates that some never-married men

> just don't like women. . . . I can be like that. I'm in the position of trying to convince women that I am worth something, and I don't think they are worth me having to do that. I don't think that I respect them all that much; I've never met one that I could work for, one who could do a job near as well as a man. I know what that sounds like, but it is just from the gut, so I hope you know I am working on it. As bosses they are picayune and inflexible, so there are times when I have negative feelings about the whole thing.

Duane's comments notwithstanding, most bachelors reflect either neutrally or positively on marriage. A few bachelors are personally indifferent to marriage, but only a small handful finds it totally without merit. This examination of bachelors' attitudes toward marriage presents them as sensible men who are not rigidly wedded to unreasonably defending their own lifestyles. Most bachelors see possible advantages in marrying, assets that they consider acquiring for themselves.

ADVANTAGES OF BEING SINGLE

I like being single because if I accomplish something, I feel like I earned it on my own, and it is more satisfying that way. (*Clyde*)

I'm 44 and I have very strong prejudices about the way I live and a great deal of freedom, and it's hard for me to imagine giving those things up. (*Curt*)

Bachelors consistently cite three chief advantages of being single:

- maintaining personal freedom and liberty,
- keeping options open, and
- avoiding problems with relationships.

Far and away the greatest advantage bachelors cite for remaining single is maintaining personal freedom and liberty. Bachelors acknowledge that marriage by its very nature redefines and alters the partners, and they do not want to risk the loss of independence and self-determination that comes with it. The specter of losing their freedom is not equal to the potential gains made through marriage. Doug slides between talking about himself and men in general when he asserts that men do not marry because

they know that it is a risky business, or they feel it to be a risky business. And I don't mean risky in the sense of some outside, objective odds, like it is risky to bet on the horses. I mean it in terms of one's own sense of integrity and identity, because if my identity and integrity are in question already, and I get married to a woman who is more sure of herself than I, then I will be drowned. I am sure that is why some men don't marry; it is partly why I haven't. And if I got married to a woman who [made demands], the terror that that brings to mind is incredible because, shit, I've just lost myself. I have just gone down the god damn drain.

Bachelors recognize that their singleness helps them avoid having to compromise their personal independence. Personal freedom is so highly valued that they are afraid marriage would be an intolerable compromise. By not marrying, they preserve what is exceedingly important to them: self-determination. Remaining single serves this definitive purpose for bachelors. Some feel there is something loathsome, regressive, or demeaning about being accountable to a spouse. So not being married is one way bachelors guard their independence. Fred states that men do not get married because "there can be a fear when there is acceptance and intimacy. You see, having someone rely on me, having someone bond with you, means a loss of autonomy."

Fred, and other bachelors, fears that being married would take away his ability to put his own stamp on his life. Other statements in this regard include Edgar's comment that "Sally was trying to make me into something I didn't want to be" and Floyd's complaint that "she would be molding me into something else." Bachelors talk of their former relationships ending because they were "losing control of [their] freedom" or "having to make too many changes" or being "told what to do." In these comments we see that the popular practice of dismissing bachelors as simply unable to commit does not appreciate the depth with which some bachelors get concerned about losing their own identity in an intimate relationship with a woman.

Bachelors have a high, perhaps exaggerated, awareness of the accountability that comes with marriage. Freedom from having to account for themselves is defended diligently. They fixate on this facet to a greater degree than they observe that the corollary to accountability is connectedness.

Some bachelors feel that the act of conferring with someone else in and of itself poses difficulties. For instance, Curt states, "I have the freedom to make my own decisions without consultation, and I have the freedom to make my own mistakes without having to worry about whether there are consequences on other people." Elmo sounds similar as he succinctly states, "I just don't have to confer with anyone else, and I am not going to trade that in for anything." To some people these men sound selfish, but are they really? Is it so bad to state precisely what you want and then set up a life in which actualizing these goals is accomplished without infringing on anyone else?

Other never-married men are concerned that wives make demands for their husbands to change. For instance, Charles states:

> I perceive women as wanting to change me. If I could find a woman who said, "You're okay the way you are," I think I would just be enraptured by that. But I have never found that in real life; I have just found women who said, "Well if you would change your hairstyle, or your clothes, or the way you live, then you'd be okay." They want to remake me. I do not want to do that. I don't want to become a camper in my own house. Any woman who wants to share my life had better know that I am my own person.

Many of these men report their early family experiences as having been stifling and constricted, so now they avoid being limited by others. For instance, Derrick reflects, "I like that I can make decisions without consulting with someone. I have the freedom to come and go as I please. I wouldn't like to have to 'check in with Mommy.' I had a lot of restrictions when I was a child and I wouldn't want that to happen again."

Edgar also shows how his family influences his current undertakings by stating, "I like my independence, the fact that I can make whatever decisions I want. The only person I need to worry about the decisions I make is my mother, and I want to keep it that way . . . and usually I ignore her." Avoiding his mother's comments demonstrates Edgar's passiveness when dealing with others. The threat of letting someone else's ideas influence his decisions feels as worrisome to this man as being locked in a closet feels to a claustrophobic person. Both individuals avoid these threatening situations. Their avoidance produces an immediate—often dramatic—reduction in anxiety, creating a feeling of well-being, which reinforces the avoidance. Therefore, the likelihood that they will choose this coping mechanism again increases.

Another aspect of accountability is compromise. Bachelors are quick to point out that being free from having to make accommodations is the best part of being single. They relate, for instance, "nothing impinges on me," "I have no constraints," "I can meet the work demands I set for myself," or "I wouldn't want to give up the hands-on operation of my business." These men fear that being married would force them to change their routine: They would have to consider the needs of others, and this would force them to modify their personal plans. They are unwilling to do so.

Ethan, with his Harley-Davidson stored for the winter in the kitchen of his small one-bedroom apartment, states, "I don't want to answer to nobody. The expectations placed on a husband by a woman are too much." Flip states, "I have a strong desire for change, and I want to be free to go with the changes." Chris, now a recovering alcoholic, used to believe that having a wife would limit his opportunity to drink, a choice he was not willing to exercise then. Eric captures the beliefs of many bachelors when he says, "Marriage would be too restrictive to my lifestyle." The implication here is that never-married men are leading some wild life. But for the most part bachelors are rather sedate. They are not carousers. Nor are they risk takers. But they want to be free to do whatever they wish.

Consistent with keeping control over their own lives is the second major advantage of being single: Remaining single is a way to keep their options open. Having alternatives in their recreational, professional, and interpersonal activities is important to bachelors. They state how much they like setting their own personal agendas. For instance, Dave states, "I can just pick up and go someplace whenever I want." Clive reflects this typical concern about keeping recreational options open: "If I want to go to the Bahamas for a weekend, I can just decide to do it, pick up and go. And I do that sometimes." Keeping his options open appears more important to Clive than actually acting on the opportunity, as he has taken only two spur-of-the-moment trips in the last ten years. Carl captures what is probably more the reality of the mixed experience of having total flexibility as he says, "I have total freedom of movement. I can decide how and what I want to do and just do it. I mean, that does get old sometimes, but it is nice to have when I want it." As is often the case in so many areas of our lives, having the option to act a certain way can be as important as actually exercising that privilege.

With regard to keeping their options open about committing to a wife, almost a third of bachelors interviewed readily admit that they are looking for a woman better than the ones they have dated in the past. "What if you finally ask a woman to marry you, and she says yes, and then the next day someone better comes along?" is Dan's lament. Curt, who was engaged, but broke it off, admits, "I have always been looking for something better." He continues his self-exploration by saying, "I wouldn't want to marry anyone who is similar to my background because I have rejected my background, so I was really looking for a very particular kind of woman."

Dave recognizes that his drive to find "the perfect woman" has modified over time as he relates his reason for remaining single:

> I was always looking for someone who was a better partner, who had more of the qualities that I was looking for. And I was always looking, and the qualities I was looking for meant someone that I would have a more satisfying, fulfilling life with. Someone who would make me feel good in more ways than the other person. And it hasn't been until the last two years that I realized there is no greener grass on the other side of the fence.

Dave seems to have come to the mature realization that refusing to see a partner as "good enough" and instead maintaining the facade of searching for the elusive "perfect" wife is just another way of avoiding commitment by denying the collaborative development possible and necessary between partners.

What these men do not understand is that good marriages are made, not found. Two people work in concert to reach their full potential both as a couple and as individuals. People who are happily married do not just *find* the perfect partner; they work for years to create a situation in which they are both productive partners for each other. The competitive trait of looking for the "perfect wife" is most common among Conflicted bachelors. Although parts of the Conflicted bachelors want to be married, they size up potential wives only to find them lacking; they keep marriage at arm's length. Always looking for something better ensures that Conflicted bachelors will not get it.

Getting along with others is not always easy. Sometimes relating involves real challenges or, worse, problems. The third advantage of being single cited by bachelors is that they avoid problems with relationships. About one-third of the bachelors interviewed say they enjoy remaining single because it helps them avoid arguing, fighting, or simply not getting along with a woman. Derrick states that couples that he has enjoyed watching over the years have been those that are "collaborators rather than sparring partners." But he notes that this phenomenon is rare, and that he has yet to find it for himself. Derrick speculates:

If things are good between you and the other person, the details, the superficial stuff, can be worked out. But if you don't find the right person, then no amount of "dressing it up" can make it better. This last relationship I was in was about the worst. We would have long arguments about anything that she didn't like. It got to the point where everything I would do was wrong. I did not enjoy the fighting and quarrels and the recriminations. There was a kind of a demand-ingness of things that I didn't want.

Dennis is more harsh as he relates that a former girlfriend "Would start these arguments, seemingly out of the blue. And I just didn't want to fight, but I can't take yelling at me from a woman, so I would get crazy and become like a volcano. . . . I hit a woman once and it was so awful; it hurt me so much, but I got pushed."

Bachelors who state that remaining single helps them avoid arguments sometimes implicate the woman as being the trigger for these events. For instance, Evan states, "she made people covet her, by being friendly and flirtatious, and that caused real prob-lems for us; we'd fight about it all the time." Eric said he could not marry because "it might be like that other relationship in which she would always put me down in public, and that was a sore spot." Dexter says that "my old girlfriends would be so demanding that I would have to fight for my own turf. I don't miss that."

However, other men admit that they are the source of the failure to not get along productively in relationships. For example, Erwin says that "I might lack the basic ingredients for getting along with others. I don't know what it is, but if I get challenged or don't like the way things are going, I can feel myself pulling away from people. I don't think I have ever worked things out; I just make the problem go away." Chris reports mixed feelings about getting along with others as he relates:

Being on my own takes off the pressure I feel to be perfect. If I felt that things were not just perfect [in the relationship], I would be very uncomfortable and become very selfish, and not my best side would come out because I would be too nervous, too uncomfortable. Then I would become resentful, too, and then we would fight about it. I'm glad I don't do that on a regular basis.

Duane takes some of the responsibility for his unpleasant experiences by stating that being in a relationship leaves him with "a real poverty mentality all the time. Like I am not worth much and I've got to convince her that I am worth something. And that was because I wouldn't be with somebody who would see me as worth something. I guess I am attracted to be with somebody I have to convince that I am worth something."

The men who identify deficiencies in their ability to get along with others range from Clyde, who observes that "I have lacked the ability to relate well enough to marry because of a certain immaturity about the way I get along," to several men who see themselves as never having been able to relate with members of the other sex in constructive, equitable terms. Conflicted bachelors are the most likely to criticize their ability to get along with others. Doug, for instance, articulates his experience, which is similar to those of other men, as he states that marriage

> has always felt like something to take on, and I don't want to take it on. It's not something that I have wanted to get into. I just don't have enough, well I certainly never had in the past, the ability to talk about my feelings so that relationships could be any good. This is changing now, slowly, but I am really having to work at it. Sharing, equally, is just hard for me to do.

Relating to women has always felt like a shortcoming for Craig. He describes the one time he considered getting married: "I developed physical symptoms. I think the idea at that time made me very uncomfortable, and immediately after, I saw a therapist. [*Author*: What was uncomfortable about considering marriage?] I don't know. I think one of my things, it is an issue I deal with now, is my own self-esteem." Struggles with self-esteem also appear to constrict the possibility of marriage for Dexter as he relates, "Dealing with my previous relationships, there's only been one relationship that I know of where I've been confident at all that the girl I was going with would marry me, and because of that, I can't say that I've ever seriously considered marriage." The challenge to one's self-esteem that occurs within a relationship is most pronounced among some of the Conflicted bachelors and will be considered more fully with that bachelor type.

Another reason that some men fear relationships is the emotional vulnerability that comes when a relationship does not work out.

Craig shows his emotional and interpersonal withdrawal to avoid this problem as he declares, "I don't want to have anything like this last one; this whole rejection thing is something that I avoid. Commitment, rejection, vulnerability, risk, and all those things. I feel that I would rather lock myself in a nice room and keep everything out and play with a computer or something." Dean's concerns are similar to Carl's and revolve around the man being left broke and broken following a marriage that did not last:

> I think in my case, I feel like, if I gave myself the way I have in relationships, it would be such a hurt if it ended. In the past it has inevitably ended. I have never had any relationships that really lasted. Had I stayed with these and pushed them, I could have gotten married, but it wouldn't have lasted. The inevitability of two people being together for life just hasn't worked for me.

Like both these men, Carl says that for him singleness helps him sidestep the pain that has been part of getting along with women: "Men don't get married because they don't want to get divorced. . . . Fifty years ago a guy could have gone out and found himself a marriage partner. Fifty years ago people didn't get divorced just like that. I don't want to get divorced. If I am going to be in it, I want to be in it."

While bachelors cite maintaining their personal freedom and liberty, keeping their options open, and avoiding problems with relationships as three primary advantages of being single, they also observe that there are shortcomings to being single.

SHORTCOMINGS OF BEING SINGLE

> I miss the fact that I have few, random social interactions. Casual, non-planned exchanges, human contact, does not occur on a daily basis. Every human contact has to be planned; it is not spontaneous and random. (Dave)

Most bachelors acknowledge that there are drawbacks to being single. The price bachelors pay for maintaining their single status revolves around four grievances:

- no one to share experiences with on a day-to-day basis,
- times of loneliness,

- lack of long-term planning and building, and
- "nagging uncertainties."

The majority of bachelors interviewed note that the worst part of not being married is having no one to share experiences with on a regular basis. They lack easy, convenient social interactions. Most of these men convey a simple wish for more interaction with another familiar person. They are not looking to share deep emotional experiences, but they have a desire for uncomplicated contact with someone they value. For instance, Dick says, "The worst part of being single for me is that there's no one to share with. It would be nice sometimes to come home to someone at night." Ernest relates, "I miss doing things with someone. Something simple can be a lot of fun, and more fun, when done with somebody else. Planting a garden, canoeing, just doing things with someone else." Cliff, a self-identified "party animal," says, "I'd like the company that would be around if I was married, someone to share with. Doing the laundry, being at home, cooking meals—it would be nice to share these things with someone else."

Bachelors report missing out on the ease of having an "assumed" companion for activities, someone they can reliably count on to participate with them. Some bachelors mention specific activities that they would increase if they were married. Ethan relates that "I would like to go to plays, but I don't want to spend a lot of money just for that one night of being together. I would like to have one woman that I could count on doing those kind of things with."

Doug, on the other hand, is more general as he laments, "Sometimes it takes a great deal of work to get a good companionship going and do things together. [Not being married] you have to build anew every time. Not being married means that there is no 'habit' of companionship, or there isn't the same 'habit' of companionship." Similarly Flip is disappointed that many of his interactions lack "history" and have an uncertain future:

What I don't like about being single is the fact that I never have anything to build on, on a permanent level. If I go to Florida or California or Europe, it sure would be nice to look back at the same gal and say "Gosh, that was great; we had such a great time." As it is, I go to these places with different women, and we can't look back on things we did together.

What many of these men miss are the easy, ordinary interactions possible when living with another person. They share the concern that Marie voiced to Sally in the movie *When Harry Met Sally*: "You broke up with Joe? How miserable—you guys were a couple. You had someone to go places with. You had a date for national holidays."

A second shortcoming of being single is occasional loneliness. Loneliness is considered the worst part of not being married by about one-third of the bachelors interviewed. Loneliness is a different experience from the desire to have shared interaction with someone else because different, deeper feelings are involved. Bachelors who mention loneliness as the worst part of being single do so emphatically, but often with little elaboration. Even the men who mention this shortcoming withdraw quickly from this emotional aspect of their lives. They offhandedly say, "Yeah, I get lonely sometimes, but. . . ." Rather than seeing discussion about their feelings as an opportunity to work out their problems, these men find these emotions too difficult to approach. This emotional avoidance compartmentalizes their feelings, but does nothing to dissipate them.

Interestingly, Flexible bachelors rarely mention either "no assumed companion" or "loneliness" as a liability of being single. They seem to manage their interpersonal needs with greater agility, so that they do not suffer the same discomfort as their Conflicted or Entrenched peers. As will be seen in the next chapter, because Flexible bachelors are better able to carry on more meaningful and longer relationships, they suffer less from social and emotional isolation and construct a more satisfying single life.

A third drawback of being single, which about one-quarter of bachelors voice, is not having a partner with whom to build a future. Fred states:

> I think the worst part [of being single], looking back, is the lack of planning in my life. This has led to uncertainty. A sense of commonality, a kind of goal orientation was not there. Although short-term planning does get projected into the future, when I dated these women, we were still missing a common sense of purpose.

Some men note the difficulty of negotiating particular personal decision points in their lives without the help and support of someone who really knows them. "Maybe if I had had someone to bounce ideas off, I could have gone a lot farther in my life," states Drake. Charles shifts from impersonal to personal when he talks of his desire to consult with someone who knows him:

> I think most people benefit from sometimes getting advice from others. When I was 30, I went without a job for almost a year. It was an awful year. I wish I had a partner then to help me consider and reconsider the possibilities. But I also miss having someone to play with ideas and make plans. Not just about jobs, but things which are more important, like getting along with others and caring for my family. That is why I have sought out a counselor to help me figure out what to do with some of these bigger questions.

Some bachelors sorely miss the prospect of having children of their own. This is one aspect of the "long-term building" made possible in marriage that bachelors miss out on. Fred relates poignantly, "My vision of Hell is an eternity of seeing the children you would have had, if you had faith and only done the right thing. And those children are all handsome or pretty, bright and energetic, and they are all smart and nice and accomplished."

As deeply as some of these men may have shared Fred's Hell, fewer than one-third of the bachelors interviewed mention having children as something important to them. Flexible bachelors are most likely to desire having their own children—perhaps because they are more settled and interpersonally adept. But some Conflicted bachelors also voice this desire. Conflicted bachelors tend to mention an interest in children, but they have some concerns about their ability to be good fathers, so their feelings can seem superficial. For instance, Chris is ambivalent about having children of his own, but he relates:

> A couple of years ago I was crossing a busy street, and there were some kids going to school. There was a little boy and his sister there, maybe 6, 7, maybe 8 years old. I started crossing the street about the same time they did. They were walking alongside of me. Some traffic was coming, and I put my arm down just to signal them to stop, and the little girl reached up and grabbed my hand. I said to myself, "Oh my God." I hadn't felt that in years. It was just the strangest feeling. It just felt so nice, one of the nicest feelings I've ever had. Innocence, trust, you know, putting faith in you. I thought, maybe there's possibilities here for me.

Felix demonstrates some of the characteristic bachelor inhibition when he states, "I would like children, but I am undecided about whether or not I will make the commitment at this time. I'm also not sure I have the temperament or the time to do it."

In contrast, having children of their own is anathema to Entrenched bachelors. For example, Ethan states, "I wouldn't have the first clue what to do with a child," and Elmo says, "My parents did a lousy job with us, and I would not want to repeat it."

"Nagging uncertainties" is the fourth disadvantage bachelors voice about being single. Persistent personal doubts weigh on the minds of about one-quarter of bachelors. Evan explains, "For me the worst part of being single is the self-incrimination and self-doubt that I wonder about. It doesn't grab me very often, but sometimes I wonder if I'm not intimate with anybody because I can't be." The self-doubt that seems to come with being single is expressed in a variety of ways, as when Derrick comments, "I wonder if there is something deficient in me for not being married"; Frank observes, "Sometimes I wonder if I would be better off married"; and Curt states, "I can feel curiously uninvolved, sometimes unnecessary, and I wonder whether it wouldn't be easier to fit into this 'married world' if I was married." Doug, too, shares his uncertainty as he relates that "there are feelings of guilt that I haven't lived up to some expectations about getting married. I have those guilt feelings, there is no denying them, and I am critical of myself, even though I think that they are unreasonable."

Expectations, spoken and unspoken, influence us. "Proper" roles are assigned by society, family, and even ourselves. When we do not fulfill these roles, we can doubt ourselves. At these times we entertain questions about our personal worth. These doubts can be mobilizing, leading to constructive change. However, for bachelors their personal insecurities, combined with emotional detachment and interpersonal passivity, seem to be limiting. Because of this, nagging uncertainties can become self-fulfilling: Our lack of confidence inhibits our performance, which then increases our self-doubt, which starts the whole process over again. This vicious cycle seems especially common among Conflicted bachelors, who have a tendency to get down on themselves. They get despondent about their lives. Notable, however, is the observation that this fourth category of the shortcomings of remaining single seems to impact only one-quarter of bachelors.

What we see in bachelors' attitudes toward marriage and in their review of the advantages and shortcomings of being single are the reasonable observations that being married can be positive and that being single has drawbacks to it. Flexible and Entrenched bachelors tend to focus more on the advantages of remaining single; they make being single work for them. Conflicted bachelors are less sure about the trade-offs. Not marrying is a legitimate option that some men exercise in order to maintain control over their lives. Not marrying is a means for bachelors to guard their independence. Not marrying also means that the possibility of failure in marriage is averted. Remaining single also keeps the host of available options uncompromised. Managing the risks and hassles of marriage by steering away from them is very important for many bachelors.

These views help clarify the personality traits and styles of interaction that are deep-seated among bachelors: Their strong need for independence, muted emotional lives, passivity when relating to others, and imprecise, idiosyncratic thinking are also seen in their marital beliefs. In addition, particularly with Conflicted bachelors, we observe nagging uncertainties about themselves and their personal abilities, which seem to reinforce their desire for independence. These features, if unchecked, can interfere with their ability to get along with others on productive, intimate levels.

Personal liberty seems foremost in the pleasures bachelors derive from not being married. Personal freedom is a highly valued commodity, which they do not want to compromise in marriage. The price most men feel they pay for protecting their distinctiveness is times of loneliness and isolation. Feeling that something is missing due to reduced interpersonal activity is reported more often among the Entrenched and Conflicted bachelors; the Flexible bachelors have more contact with others, so that they do not report the same isolation as the other men. Flexible bachelors, however, are not free from paying a price for their freedom. For them the price is not having children of their own.

The general personality traits described in the last chapter and illustrated through their views of marriage in this chapter, play out quite differently in the three bachelor types. The psychology of bachelors cannot be fully appreciated until each of these categories and divisions is delineated in the three chapters that follow.

5

FLEXIBLE BACHELORS: A QUESTION OF PRIORITIES

All bachelors have a strong commitment to self-determination. They value self-reliance and organize their lives so that other people do not interfere with their independence. Even the women they care about threaten their freedom. Marriage presents a great challenge to their autonomy, so they steer a wide path around it. To a greater or lesser degree, all bachelors tend to keep their emotions at a distance, they all avoid situations that will evoke strong feelings, and they all can misread people and situations through their idiosyncratic reasoning. These styles of relating, which are their defenses, maintain their individuality. However, some bachelors are more adept at getting along with others. Their protective ways of interacting are less automatic, less pervasive, and more yielding.

Flexible bachelors are the ones who demonstrate the most ability to relax their internal protective tactics. They are called "Flexible" because they adjust their internal defenses and external behaviors in order to interact more comfortably and productively. Compared with other bachelors, Flexible bachelors are more social and less ambivalent about getting along with others. They also tend to be more satisfied with their lives. Flexible bachelors can relate well to others when they choose to. They have deeper and longer relationships with women. They are able to be more interdependent. Flexible bachelors are more likely to be confident regarding themselves and their abilities. These men are still bachelors, traveling their life paths in solitary fashion, but their versatility means that they are more accomplished and more fulfilled.

Flexible bachelors make up about a quarter of all bachelors. Flexible bachelors' personal accomplishments make them stand out from the other bachelor types. They are likely to have higher incomes, be professional, have more years of education, and own their residences. Many successfully run their own businesses or are effective professionals. Because they are comfortable, few Flexible bachelors seek psychotherapy. The choices they have made for themselves keep them generally satisfied with their lives, and they do not feel the need to change.

Flexible bachelors create their independent lifestyle out of a benign indifference to marriage rather than as an apprehensive reaction to and retreat from women. These men could have gotten married, but instead their priorities led them to make other choices. People are important to Flexible bachelors, but instead of relationships being paramount, other activities mattered more. For some Flexible bachelors finishing their professional training or establishing themselves in their professions was given first priority. Others took on caring for their aging parents as a primary task. Many men do these same things and also get married, but the bachelors decided that accomplishing these tasks was best done on their own. This attitude seemed to delay their commitment to marriage, a delay that they maintain out of familiarity and comfort.

Flexible bachelors expect that they will get married; they just have not gotten around to it yet. However, of the three types Flexible bachelors are second to Conflicted men in their likelihood of getting married. Although their achievements and their abilities to enjoy love with women may make them look like the most eligible bachelors to wed, Flexible bachelors are not longing for marriage. Flexible men are pleased with the lives they have built for themselves. They are content. The typical hesitancy of most bachelors, when combined with Flexible men's overall life-satisfaction, means that they feel no sense of urgency to tie the knot. This cluster of men does not have the personality disturbances of Entrenched bachelors, who are so rigidly wedded to their defenses that they exclude meaningful relationships. Nor are Flexible bachelors as torn between independence and loneliness as are Conflicted men.

Of the three bachelor types Flexible bachelors look like they would make the best husbands. In general, they are more entertaining, social, easygoing, and caring than their Conflicted or Entrenched counterparts. Despite all these attributes, Flexible bachelors feel that remaining single is the best way to maintain their integrity. Although their self-confidence is real and significant, maintaining these feelings depends at least in part on remaining detached from others.

The families Flexible bachelors grew up in appear to be the base for their confidence and positive self-opinions. Flexible bachelors describe their families in positive terms such as "very child-centered," "supportive," "loving," "stable and secure," and "close-knit." Unlike so many other bachelors, Flexible bachelors are more likely to describe their parents' marriages as happy. Flexible bachelors see themselves as similar to other members of their families, so they have a strong base of support and positive role models.

Some Flexible bachelors report constructive competition in their families. For instance, Flip says, "My brother and I were constantly trying to outdo each other. He always managed to outperform me in the classroom, but I was always the better athlete. It was good that we each had our own areas in which to excel." This type of competitiveness made a deep impression on these men, perhaps to the point where measurable success gained preeminence over less tangible accomplishments such as relationships. For instance, Flip is proud of the extraordinary success of his restaurant, but acknowledges that his brother has succeeded in raising his own family.

Flexible bachelors are still single, though, and profess with pride their social and emotional independence. Dependent and needy feelings are difficult for these men to tolerate. This is consistent with the teachings from the families in which they grew up. Interdependence, relying on another and in turn being relied on, is threatening because sharing responsibility may lead to failure. Success is something to be achieved by an individual, not a couple. In addition, victories are diminished if they are part of a team effort. Flexible bachelors value success and recognition (unlike Entrenched bachelors), but they may consider trading in their individual achievements for the potential gains to be made in sharing their lives through marriage. Although they think about marrying, they are too busy to muse and fret about it the way Conflicted bachelors do.

Flexible men are also different from other bachelors because they describe the women they have dated in terms of the love and affection they felt and the growth they experienced. They describe their lives as intertwined with others rather than parallel to them. They have had a greater number of romantic relationships than either Conflicted or Entrenched bachelors. Their average age of sexual initiation was younger than those of the other bachelor groups, and they describe their sexual experiences as being more positive. They are not casual about sex, instead seeing it as an aspect of a loving relationship. Flexible bachelors say that having children is of interest to them. All these interpersonal behaviors are indicative of Flexible bachelors' ability to relate productively with others.

Two extended examples will clarify how these men live, interact, and define themselves in ways common to Flexible bachelors and different from the other two types of bachelors.

DESCRIPTIVE CASE STUDIES

Frank and Fred are men whose personal characteristics exemplify many of the life-structure patterns of the Flexible bachelor personality cluster.

Frank is a 41-year-old man, born and raised in a midwestern farming community. Standing about six feet three inches tall, Frank has the natural, healthy, rugged good looks of a midwesterner. He has been employed for 12 years as a college professor at a small, rural college in Michigan. His guardedness was evident when we first met: Instead of talking in his college office, he ushered me down the hall to a stark, impersonal meeting room. More comfortable during our second interview, Frank invited me into his office, which was filled with personal memorabilia, university degrees, and pictures from various trips. While this second meeting place offered more personal impressions of Frank, it was still not the same as having been invited into his home. At all times during our interaction Frank was friendly, thoughtful, and forthcoming, but careful in what he said. He always used a staccato delivery, which was consistent with his pragmatic, no-nonsense speaking style.

Frank spent two years in the armed forces after graduating from college. He felt that these years were a waste of time and talent.

He left the service wondering if he "had lost the intellectual edge." Consequently he began graduate school with a sense of "foreboding," which led to his pouring himself into his studies and ignoring relationships. His priority was completing his Ph.D. in mathematics so that he could establish himself professionally. This emphasis on his professional development continued into his early 30s. During this time he dated occasionally, but always with the idea that his studies came first. Even so, he began his teaching career before completing his Ph.D. and for five years had his "dissertation looming overhead."

Frank was obviously very good at teaching, earning tenure the same year he completed his dissertation and received his degree. He has also won several teaching awards. Teaching is very important to Frank's personal identity:

> I would describe myself as a committed teacher, committed to helping people learn and reach their potential. I am a perfectionist and a skeptic, and this helps me in the classroom. My greatest achievement has been in becoming an excellent teacher, and I know that I am from the student reviews that I get. I am pleased that I can influence a lot of lives.

Although he chose teaching because it afforded him the opportunity to be involved with others, mathematics does not require the emotional responsiveness that might more automatically develop in fields like psychology or literature.

Consistent with Frank's desire to help others, he came to my attention through a mutual colleague and volunteered for the study out of personal interest and a desire to help with my research. Helping others is something that Frank saw in his family when he was growing up. Frank identifies with his family, which he describes as having "a sense of love and support." He is the oldest of the five children, who are "an interesting bunch, competitive, but not in a negative way. We were all very bright, and we had very good parents who taught us responsibility and accountability, but also taught us to use what we were given and to fully participate in life. I look back fondly on the years with my family."

Describing his parents' marriage as "stable, secure, and supportive," Frank wants that same kind of partnership for himself. Observing similarities between himself and his father, Frank states, "We have the same drive, the same high standards for ourselves.

And in some ways we have the same impatience with foolishness. What's the phrase, 'someone who does not suffer fools gladly.' We don't put up with much." Frank notes that his father tended to dominate his wife, something Frank did not like. Frank insists that he and his wife would "work to make the relationship more equal between the two of us," a statement that illustrates Frank's thoughtfulness about marriage and his belief that he can effectively create better relationships than he has seen. Frank also developed a "very loving and patient" side, which he feels is like his mother. These feelings led to his desire to be involved in a serious relationship.

Not having a family of his own is specifically and unequivocally his biggest disappointment with life. His regret about his lack of family is apparent, especially when he states, "In my life I am most disappointed in not finding someone to live with and make a personal commitment to share lives. I'm still looking, optimistic and expecting. But that's one of the drawbacks of a smaller town, in that the number of contacts is reduced."

During his adulthood Frank had been involved in three serious relationships: one during graduate school, two during his teaching years. He considers them "serious" because they involved "deeply caring about her well-being. Wanting her to be happy, to enjoy life and get better at what she does and at who she is. Wanting that and being a partner. They were mutual. In a serious relationship you have to have that part reciprocated." His most recent relationship was a several-year involvement with a woman who had a professional position in another part of the country. He says this relationship was very positive. He enjoyed the caring, trust, and confidences they had and the mutuality they achieved. However, as in all three of his serious relationships, their individual commitments led to the deterioration of the relationship. "We lived too far apart to continue, and our careers kept us apart."

Frank is frustrated that this most recent relationship ended, but he feels nothing could be done about it. "I don't like it when my desires for closeness and sharing are unsuccessful or go unreciprocated. That may sound like it is on a physical level, but I also mean on a personal level." This imbalance typically ends his relationships. Frank identified the worst part of relationships as "cases in which I was eager to bond more, to reveal more of myself and wanted to know more of her, but she wasn't ready to do likewise. I am not very comfortable with someone who has chosen not to develop that relationship between us, so that is generally toward the end of our contact; that is the beginning of the end."

Frank says he became sexual later than his peers, although his age of first intercourse was 19. When reflecting on the sexual aspects of his last relationship, he said that "sex in the context of a relationship is fabulous, a facet of the bonding and mutual interest that I long for. Making love brought so much life to both of us. I don't have enough of that kind of sharing." At the same time he is not driven by the need for sexual outlets, stating that "I have dated some women for months without sexual relations. We stop dating before we really got that involved." His mature abilities to relate are evident in his healthy statements about sexual expression, but some of his passivity is noted in his statement that "not having sex wasn't for the lack of hope on my part."

Frank would like to be married. He feels ready now that his career is in place. He is confident that he could have a good marriage with the right woman, "who would respect the demands of my work." In this last statement we see his need to hold onto areas of life that are exclusively his. He still likes being single because it allows him to take an independent approach to his career and to invest more fully in his professional undertakings. He fears that being married would force him to cut back on his personal activities, but he is now more willing to do so in order to achieve the companionship that he desires.

> The worst part of not being married is that I have had to do it on my own. But that has also allowed me to achieve certain goals. The lack of companionship has been notable and at times, especially in the last five or six years, I get lonely. I would like to have a wife and children. I am fascinated by seeing and being part of learning and developing.

Notably Frank began to experience an increased loneliness and longing for marriage after he completed his dissertation. Having finished one achievement, it appears that Frank was ready to move on with other areas of his life. However, although he says he is looking for "that someone special," his relationships with women are more activity based and casual at this time: "I miss a real companion in a real, sharing, committed way—someone with whom I could make plans and build on something over time. Not just someone accompanying you, in the same location with you, but someone with whom you can really share experiences and live life together."

Frank is "reasonably certain" that he will get married. He worries that an opportunity will not present itself, or that his tendency toward "perfectionism" will inhibit taking action. Getting married, however, is not a goal in itself: Frank sees it as a means to his goal. "I don't need to be married to prove something to others. I just think you can gain a quality relationship within the institution, and it makes having children legal." In graduate school he had been asked by a woman with whom he was involved to get married, but "I couldn't at the time. And, besides, we were not a good fit, so I am very glad that I said no."

Although still somewhat uncomfortable about approaching others, Frank is trying to be more open with both men and women. He sees that friendships with men are becoming more important to him, and he is working to be more successful with them by trying to be more forthcoming personally: "I have been trying to be more direct in seeking friendships and emotional intimacy. The last few years I have tried to share more of my feelings with the women I have dated, and I have tried to connect with colleagues, male and female, here on campus." He also says that going to professional conferences has become increasingly important to him "as a way to try to connect myself with other people in my field." Friendships with men are opportunities for Frank to "commiserate and celebrate." The couple of individuals with whom Frank currently feels closest and "shares matters of deep concern" are men.

Frank is overall very positive about his activities and accomplishments as he describes his adult life as

> sort of a relaxed, sightseeing trip—one that wasn't tightly planned by itinerary. Sightseeing in the sense of discovery, as if I am going to places I haven't seen before. I look at things in a discovery kind of way, I am intrigued by the new, and I am fascinated by different things. As I have gotten further along in my professional career, my focus has gotten a little narrower, but it's not limited to those topics.

Frank's analogy for his adult development is appropriate, including his self-characterization as a sightseer rather than a participant. He is discovering, but he conveys a sense of himself more as an observer than an explorer.

Where Frank is a very direct individual, Fred, another Flexible bachelor, is more elusive and roundabout. Fred has a rather dry wit, which is amusing and engaging, but also sharp-edged. For instance, Fred used quick, forceful terms to describe himself: "I have the three S's: I am straight, single, and solvent. And maybe we should add to that 'uninfected.'" Fred uses his wit to keep others at arm's length, which is consistent with the way he responded to my follow-up question about what he meant by "uninfected": "I meant virally. I am leading a clean life." Fred says, "I have no idea how others would describe me. Maybe the same, but I don't ask them, so I can't guess. I'm not so concerned with them and their opinions." Fred showed some apparent indifference to my schedule by standing me up for two different interviews we had scheduled.

Avoidance and emotional detachment may underlie Fred's indifference. They also were evident in Fred's handling of the Rorschach inkblot test, designed to tap into his internal dynamics. Although he is very bright and well educated with advanced degrees in both business and law, when faced with the uncertainty of the task, he "froze" on the Rorschach cards. He was unsettled and had a very difficult time responding to the lack of structure when asked to say what the ambiguous inkblots might be. His "freeze" suggested that he is a man with unimaginative problem-solving strategies. Fred offered fewer responses than most adults, and his answers were simple, economical, and rudimentary, just like his three-word self-description.

These responses and others suggest that Frank tends to avoid emotionally toned situations, is more guarded than most adults, and has trouble relaxing in the face of uncertainty. Fred's unconscious reaction to feeling challenged on the Rorschach test was threefold. First, he "circled his wagons" by offering mostly stark and dry descriptions of the cards. He felt threatened by having little control over what he revealed about himself. Second, he used humor as a defense against his anxiety, making statements such as "Send over the guys with the white coats" and "I hope you are enjoying this." Third, he flung the cardboard cards back at me after responding to them, revealing his potential to become hostile in response to feeling challenged and unsure.

This is the internal world of Fred, which may seem rather disturbing, but the truth is that Fred probably has many friends who look forward to his company. The external Fred is active, quick-witted, and well read. He is a tall, good-looking man who keeps fit by playing tennis a couple of nights a week. His work involves traveling around the country in addition to putting in many hours at the office, but he says he takes time to keep up with local and national sports. He keeps a clean, comfortable home, furnishing it with expensive contemporary furniture, some antiques, and a few high-quality paintings. Born and raised in Boston, Fred is 42 years old. He is the middle of three sons in his Irish Catholic family. He has been living on the Gold Coast in downtown Chicago for the past 12 years. An employee assistance consultant at a medium-sized consulting firm, his income is about $125,000. He loves the work and the income, though he hopes to "make it bigger" in the next few years. His employment makes direct use of the graduate degrees in business and law that he received when he was 30. He is quite sociable, providing snacks and beverages for both of us when we conducted the interviews at his condominium.

Fred is thoughtful and reflective in answering questions about his life. He is more expansive when talking about his family and work; more cryptic when talking about himself and his relationships. For instance, when discussing women with whom he has been involved, Fred has a difficult time defining what makes a relationship serious. He tends to distance himself from his statements by using third-person pronouns (e.g., "Well, some people would say a significant relationship is when you get physically involved. Other people would say it is how long you stay together. I'm not sure for myself"). Fred has been in five or six relationships he would label as "serious," but says, "I don't know if I have ever been in love or not." Each relationship was different from the others, but he notes that all the women were very attractive. He enjoys the companionship of women; the time spent talking and doing activities together is valued. Over the years he has had girlfriends who "used my home as if it was their own, but I've never really lived with anyone."

Not all of Fred's serious relationships have involved sexual intercourse. In fact, Fred first had sex at age 27, explaining that his Catholic upbringing led him to believe that sex outside of marriage was not acceptable. He has a hard time reconciling his sexual activity with his religious upbringing, but justifies himself by saying, "I don't do 'recreational screwing.' I have to care about the person, and we have to have some history together. When we have that, everything goes great. I used to have more guilt about sex when I felt I was not going to marry the woman."

Fred has considered marriage a couple of times and planned to ask one woman to marry him, but did not. "I was always busy and just never really got around to it. Then we seemed to miss this 'window of opportunity' and never really talked about it again." He wonders if he is awful for having "wasted her time" when he had no plans of marrying a woman he was with. Characteristically sarcastic, he explains:

> The basic reason why I am not married is that God has been very good to me. Actually that sounds rather callous, but it is true. There were a couple I look back on, and I think, "Hey, maybe she was the one." It might have been a short consumption with people; I was consumed by being with them, but as time went on, my attitude changed. And I am very lucky. Sometimes now I get information about some of the girls I dated. I know that one is completely nuts. The other most serious one married a guy she was dating when she met me and has severe, severe leukemia. And the guy treats her like shit, and she's trapped because she needs his medical insurance. And with the health problems, you know, she's just . . . I mean it's catastrophic for her, but she's miserable company. And if I had gotten my wish in May of 1979, I'd be dealing with that now. I might be better for her than her current husband, but on the whole it was a pretty good deal for me.

Fred has an interesting view, which allows him to remain distant from his feelings of marriage:

> Since I was 25 or 26, I've always assumed that in two years I'd be married. See, it goes like this: Even though I can't think of anybody today, in six months I'll meet somebody, and that'll be the one I've been looking for, and we'll have a reasonable courtship for several months, and I'll try to move prudently 'cause I don't want to be stupid about things—it's an important commitment—but in 24 months from now, I believe I could be married. Of course, I haven't been right so far.

Fred's attitudes make him sound different from a traditional stereotype of a "confirmed" bachelor committed to his independence, but his actions argue otherwise. He is not single because of an aversion to marriage or a sexual dislike of women. But neither is he drawn to marriage or sexual intimacy. He thinks he is single simply because his plans have not aligned with someone else's. Fred states that "marriage is irrelevant to the way I want to live my life now." He describes the period from age 22 to 29, a time when most men are getting married, as a time when "I was getting ready for the profession. I went to school for my master's degree, and I knew that I had to work hard to succeed. Then at 25 I got very frustrated, and I said to myself 'I'm not making enough money, and if I keep this up, I won't be able to make enough in the years to come.' "

Like many Flexible bachelors, fulfilling his ambition has been more important than committing to a relationship. Also, as they have set their sights on getting their advanced degrees, they have wanted to do so on their own. Fred puts it quite simply and represents many of the attitudes of Flexible bachelors as he states:

> Why haven't I gotten married? Well, I have had things to do. I had four years of college, my master's degree, four years of law school. You know, in 1976 or so I was in a serious relationship for about seven months. I thought this would be my wife, but then I moved away to take a new job, and the relationship took a quick turn downhill as I became consumed by the new challenges I was facing.

The emotional distancing typical of many bachelors is evident in the ease with which Fred left his girlfriend and got involved in work and other activities.

Fred's commitment to hard work and achievement is rooted in the family in which he grew up. Fred is the middle of three boys in his family, all born two years apart. His parents remained married to each other until his father died five years ago. They were older than most people when they married: His father was 35, his mother 27. "My father had waited until 35 to marry because when he was in his early 20s, the Depression hit, and he didn't have any money to get married." Fred tells a story about his father that is quite revealing about both men.

> In 1928 my father had rented a field out in South Dakota. He was trying to do his best to stay afloat in the Depression, and he felt farming a wheat field could do it. He rented the vehicles he used to plant it and then grew it. It came time to harvest the field. Whatever

that time is, you've got to harvest it when it's ready, or you miss out on everything. Well, one night he made one harvesting pass on the rented combine, with the gas he had borrowed money to get, and he made one pass, and it was clear the field was ready to yield a productive harvest. So he got ready to do the harvesting first thing in the morning. But that night he got wiped out by a localized hailstorm. The storm hit him and just flattened the field. Once it's flat, you can't harvest it. So in 1928 he's 26, and he is $8,000 in debt. That was Depression dollars. He had stood to make $25,000, he believed, on that wheat field. Well, he took the train out of town the next night and went to New England where his sister was a nurse. And for the next I-don't-know-how-many years he was paying back those dollars to the people who had trusted him in South Dakota. And he did pay it back. A few years before he died, he went out to that town in South Dakota and visited, and those people remembered him. But that was why he was not married before; there was no money to get married.

Fred's story exemplifies the prominent place hard work, honesty, and loyalty have in his life. The story is revealing about Fred because he chose it from among a myriad of family memories, vividly recounting it when discussing attitudes about marriage, and because he identifies himself as being very similar to his father.

While his father is described as dedicated and hard-working, Fred's mother is "emotional and good-hearted; she was the smartest of the five of us." When he considers his parents' marriage, Fred sits back and says:

My mother was smarter than my father, and so they didn't always see things the same, and this led to battles as they went along. That may be a fact that has influenced me to stay single. They had a tough time with each other. Not that they fought all the time, but things were always contentious. She could have married a chemical engineer who was Protestant, but instead she held out for a Catholic and married my dad. I think that bugged her until the day he died; it really bugged her.

Fred distances himself from the emotional openness this recollection brought to him by leaning over to my tape recorder and humorously adding, "Hey, I wouldn't want a shrink to get hold of that one."

Strong Catholic prohibitions against divorce and a common philosophy on raising their children were the elements that Fred believes kept his parents married for 39 years. Together they were able to transmit positive attitudes to their sons.

> My family was middle class and *real*. My father, I remember, made $24,000 in 1961. That's probably around $75,000 today, maybe a little higher. That wasn't bad, but we always lived modestly. We had a new house every few years, but never out of the same neighborhood, and always very modest. The emphasis was placed on education and using what abilities you have to move yourself along. The real emphasis was not on achieving, though there was some of that, but it was more on doing your best. They did a good job with all of us.

Fred also recognizes that his family had weaknesses: "In classic Irish Catholic fashion communication was probably not as strong or direct as it should have been." He offers the following example of this pattern:

> I remember I was on the cross-country team when I was a junior in high school. It was a very good team—so good that one of the guys went on to the Olympic team; he was that good. We were running a meet at Harvard stadium and along the Charles River. My parents asked me if I wanted them to give me a ride to the meet, and then they could stay and watch. I said, "No." I didn't want them to go to the meet. And they said, "Okay," and it was dropped. My own thought as I look back is that there are a lot of parents who would have asked, "Why don't you want us to go see you run? What's the matter?" But in my family it was just dropped. Everybody said, "Okay," and it was dropped just like that. It's a small thing, but I think if I was the parent, I would have wanted to go, and I think most kids would want their parents there. So why does this kid say no? There were probably many things we could have said that we should have, but we couldn't talk. Irish Catholics are great sulkers and great pouters, but does the Irish Catholic male talk to the Irish Catholic female? . . . Nah.

To gain more insight into Fred, I asked, "Why did you say no to your parents?" His answer reveals aspects of his competitiveness and the private approach he takes to his experiences:

> I think I feared that if we were going to lose, I didn't want them to see that; I wanted to do it on my own. And at that age you didn't have the perception that your parents would be thrilled just to see

you run. The kids think the parents want to see them win; most parents are just sort of delighted to see their kid healthy out there.

Fred is uncomfortable about making mistakes, and if he does trip up, he wants to keep that to himself.

Fred has obviously given consideration to what the role of being a father would entail. He has strong feelings about raising children of his own. "Raising children of my own scares the shit out of me. It's a massive commitment. Secondly, if it doesn't turn out well, you've just fucked something up. That may be a reason why I haven't married." Fred's passivity shows when he continues by saying, "I really have not had the overriding desire from within for fatherhood, and I haven't met the woman who has convinced me that I should stop worrying about it and just do it." Fred says he also has not met the women who said, "Hey, I don't want to have children either" and really meant it. Fred's concern about making mistakes and having them exposed comes up again as he relates:

I think the decision to get married is a far less troublesome decision than the decision to have kids. If you screw up your marriage, you've just screwed up each other for a while, but if you screw up your kids, you've unleashed something upon society whose repercussions you don't even know. A child, you know, has a life of his own. I have a lot of respect for people who raise nice kids; it ain't easy, pal, especially today.

Fred relates what a wonderful job his older brother is doing raising his three children. His mixed feelings about having children of his own are revealed as he offers, "My vision of Hell is an eternity of seeing the children you would have had, if only you had gaith and done the right thing. And those children are all handsome or pretty, bright and energetic, and they are all smart and nice and accomplished."

Fred laments that he does not have more friends in Chicago. He feels that the past eight years since he moved there to take his current professional position did not give him the opportunity to form the same kinds of friendships that he had established in other areas.

I had some friends in Washington, D.C., from my years in law school. And I have one or two great friends in New York City from the years we were all single and working together there. You know, softball every Monday night at 6:30; rent a beach house together for three months on Long Island. How can you repeat those experiences? When I got to Chicago, I was 34. When you are 25 and lots of people are single, that is one thing. When you are 35, most of them are already married and raising kids and stuff. Its been tough to come here and be without guys that I can just drop in and do things with. One of my best friends in New York has never been married, and I think it is because he scares the girls off because he wants to be married so bad. For me it has been more of a process of "there are things I'd rather do first."

Fred was socially adept throughout his interviews, although he often talked about himself indirectly. He is bright and engaging and has a sense of humor. His work is personally gratifying, and he feels he is contributing to his organization and the welfare of others, which is important to him. However, as he speaks about himself, many of his responses seemed rehearsed and overly prepared. With few exceptions his ready answers do not convey deep feelings. He avoids getting too close to emotion. His interaction style is elusive as shown in his response to my invitation: "If you look at your adult life as a trip, how would you describe your journey?" He stated, "I have no idea what the destination is. I do know that I have a desire to move on and be different from others. I also know that I have focused more on leaving and moving than on staying and putting down roots." Leaving is easier for Fred than staying.

UNDERSTANDING THE FLEXIBLE BACHELOR

Frank and Fred are examples of Flexible bachelors, men who value a life of individualism and self-reliance, but who also relate well to others. They remain reserved and emotionally detached when involved with others, but these patterns do not have the same tenacious hold on Flexible men as they do on the other types of bachelors because these men are less reliant on social and emotional distancing to maintain their psychological well-being. But the defenses are still present: Frank held a distance by keeping me out of his office; Fred was even more avoidant by not talking so much about himself, even when asked directly. Frank's emotional detachment was present in his removed, objective descriptions of his old girlfriends, while Fred's commitment lay in the direction of money rather than people.

Both bachelors demonstrated, although less than the other two types, an idiosyncratic understanding of their worlds: Frank imagined that if he were in a bigger city, he would be married, while Fred embraced the fantasy that "I've always assumed that in two years I'd be married." These distortions do not accurately reflect reality. In this vein another Flexible bachelor states, "My friends say I am a person who walks to his own beat." This observation could be made of most Flexible bachelors, who are not very different from other men—they are not disturbed—but remain uncommitted to the usual social custom of marriage.

Flexible bachelors are satisfied with their lives and their activities. They are more self-sufficient and less self-doubting than Conflicted bachelors, more socially adept than Entrenched bachelors. Frank and Fred each maintains a healthy self-opinion that is realistically rooted in each man's ability to interact with women in positive ways. They have not actively sought to be single, but their passivity in relationships, subdued emotional connectedness, and commitment to other goals have allowed each man to drift into his current bachelor state. Fred captured succinctly the position of many Flexible bachelors when he stated that "marriage is irrelevant to the way I want to live my life now."

Flexible bachelors have a high regard for women, holding them in esteem and enjoying their companionship. Their serious relationships usually involve monogamous, multi-year interactions. They enjoy sex within these relationships, but they are not driven by sexual desire. Neither Frank nor Fred ever proposed to a woman, but both had been infatuated enough to think about it. However, as Fred said, "I lose interest over time, and things get to be more difficult, and it is easier to not do anything different." Getting older has not increased their need to get married; instead, they are making the best of their single status.

Frank and Fred both wish for more male friends and work toward positive relationships with other men, both common experiences among Flexible bachelors. Most of their friendships are activity-based, and this communion with other men is extremely important. Flexible bachelors seem to be making meaningful and gratifying professional contributions, and this also appears to be a personal priority.

Typical of Flexible bachelors, Frank and Fred stay in touch with their families. Their relatives are important to them, and they talk respectfully of them. Flexible bachelors' families provide a solid, but competitive, base from which they grow. These qualities seem to enhance these men's high need for personal achievements and also give them the means to make this possible. In addition, waiting to be established professionally before marrying seems to be supported in the family patterns in which Flexible bachelors grew up. Another common pattern in their families was that their parents were older than most people when they married, therefore modeling this behavior for their sons.

The worst part of not being married for most Flexible bachelors is not having children of their own. Their concern is less about having good relationships with women—which they feel they do achieve—than it is about the responsibilities of raising a family of their own. They are extremely concerned about the restrictions that having children brings, and they worry about the individual freedom that would be lost by such a venture. Having a family of their own has taken a back seat to other concerns for most of their adult lives; as Frank says, "It has only been in the last few years, since I have managed to get the other aspects of my life to a level of comfort, that having children has become a priority."

Although attracted to marriage, Flexible bachelors are concerned that a committed relationship with a woman might impose unacceptable obstructions to individuality. They feel free because they are on their own. "You know, most women want to mold men into what they want; they won't let good enough alone" was Fred's way of articulating this position. The Flexible bachelor is not sure whether trading in his sense of individual achievement would be worth the gains made in sharing his life with someone else, and so he is reluctant to seek out a spouse. At the same time Flexible bachelors are not consumed by these questions in the ways that haunt Conflicted bachelors, leaving them dissatisfied and unhappy. Entrenched bachelors, in strong contrast to these other two bachelor types, are sure that a key to their happiness is to steer clear of marriage.

6

Entrenched Bachelors: The Pattern of Rigidity

Entrenched bachelors, the second bachelor type, are probably the unmarried men that come to mind when most people think of bachelors. They most closely fit the negative stereotype of an odd man set in his ways, indifferent to the world around him. Entrenched bachelors cling rigidly to their defenses in order to resolutely maintain their independence. And why not? Entrenched bachelors are satisfied with their lives. They are content with their self-sufficiency, even though they are the most inhibited and restrained bachelor type.

Edgar, for example, is an Entrenched bachelor who is so indifferent to social norms that he has no pictures or other wall decorations on any of his beige apartment walls. When asked about this, he just shrugs it off and says, "I haven't thought about it much," even though he has lived there for seven years. He may be so inhibited that he goes to this length to ensure that he is not being stimulated. And one has to wonder if other visitors have commented on this condition. Perhaps they have not said anything, or maybe he has no visitors. Equally possible is that he is totally indifferent to comments if they were made.

Entrenched bachelors may make up as much as a quarter of all bachelors, but it is hard to tell because Entrenched bachelors withdraw into their own private worlds. They live hermetically sealed lives. This makes them hard to count. Entrenched bachelors fade into the woodwork and do not make waves. They are content with the status quo. They are indifferent not only to marriage, but also to most areas of their lives.

Entrenched bachelors are fortified in the usual bachelor defenses. Not only do they practice emotional detachment and lack deep feelings, but also their emotional reactions may be peculiar if expressed. Their passive withdrawal takes the form of seclusion, so that they keep to themselves. Entrenched bachelors not only have a hard time correctly reading situations, but also sometimes misrepresent interpersonal interactions. They are likely to entertain vague, imprecise, and idiosyncratic observations about others, so that social relations are strained. For example, Elmo was surprised when two different women where he worked took him aside to say that he was paying too much undue attention to them and that they wanted to be left alone. He thought they had been leading him on. Entrenched bachelors are anchored in their single status because they rely on separateness to maintain themselves. Their inflexible and consistent commitment to self-determination leads to social isolation. However, even though others would not want to switch places with them, Entrenched bachelors tend to report that they are content and satisfied.

Entrenched bachelors' satisfaction with self-sufficiency gives further evidence that there are various personality types. Although their contentment is similar to that of Flexible bachelors, Entrenched bachelors are complacent out of indifference to others. Where Flexible bachelors ably maintain positive relationships to keep themselves comfortable, Entrenched bachelors' unemotional and sometimes peculiar ways exclude meaningful relationships. But not having others in their lives is not a problem for Entrenched bachelors because, more so than the other two bachelor types, they have a diminished desire for social relationships. Since they are not hungry for relatedness the way Conflicted bachelors are, Entrenched bachelors do not care that they are on paltry diets; they do not suffer the confused, mixed feelings that Conflicted bachelors have about their single status.

Entrenched bachelors are passive and lack strong conviction. They may be vague about their goals and indecisive in their actions. Others might refer to them as eccentric, although less kind people would call them strange. These are shy men who withdraw from deep relationships and are inhibited in their ability to express their feelings. One 48-year-old Entrenched bachelor interviewed was still a virgin. Like him, most Entrenched bachelors are not eager to carry on social encounters, and that is a good thing because of the three bachelor types Entrenched men are the most limited in their capacity to form positive social relationships based on warm, tender feelings for others. They steadfastly avoid situations that will evoke feelings, which limits their productive interaction with anyone, male or female. Entrenched bachelors define relationships solely in terms of instrumental activities, doing things with others rather than having feelings for them or sharing affection. For instance, an Entrenched bachelor is more apt to say a person is a friend because they are both Civil War buffs rather than because they have shared deep conversation. Entrenched bachelors also tend to be indifferent to praise, criticism, and the feelings of others.

Even though Entrenched bachelors can be asocial and lack compassion, they are not dangerous. They are not likely to strike out against others because within their cloistered worlds they get their needs met, so they do not care about much else. Entrenched men may show an initial interest in sex when relating to a woman, maybe for several dates, but they either have a low sex drive or are too out of touch with their feelings to sustain this interest. Their ability to experience sexual desire is directly linked to their sense of personal autonomy. That is, if they feel their independence encroached on, their desire for sex will diminish or may stop altogether. Entrenched bachelors may be less frustrating to women who might be attracted to them than are the other types of bachelors because they are more consistent than Conflicted bachelors in stating their lack of intention to get seriously involved with a woman and are less socially intriguing than Flexible bachelors. Entrenched bachelors have no desire to become fathers themselves.

Entrenched bachelors are noteworthy because, in spite of their limitations, they are not in distress. They show little or no desire for social involvement. Disengagement is far more satisfying to them than trying to get along with others. Entrenched bachelors accept their current status without complaint and are content with themselves and their lives to a greater degree than many men—married or single. Entrenched bachelors establish a congenial balance between their personal needs and the way in which they relate to their world. The intrapsychic processes of the Entrenched bachelors, while possibly closing them off to rich experiences in their lives, are maintaining them at a level of personal comfort.

At times Entrenched bachelors' behavior looks similar to that of the other bachelor types, but the motivations underlying their actions are quite different. For instance, an Entrenched bachelor's lack of resolute, goal-directed activity is often seen in a Conflicted bachelor, but simply not caring underlies the Entrenched bachelor's actions, while perplexed consternation constricts the Conflicted man. Likewise, although the Entrenched bachelor's self-absorbed detachment may look similar to that of the Flexible bachelor, the Entrenched bachelor must actively separate himself from others; the Flexible man acts more out of choice.

Bachelors in the Entrenched personality cluster seem to learn their patterns of relating in the families in which they grew up. They talk of their families as "constricting," "independent and differentiated," "contentious," "showing limited lovingness and affection," and "having limited communication." In general, Entrenched men report minimal human interaction in their homes when growing up, and some recognize that emotional expression was squelched. When their parents are not described as cold and unaffectionate, they are usually shrouded in mystery: They are "unknown" or "hidden." This background begins to explain why these men would be satisfied and comfortable with their low social interaction. Whether, of course, their recollections of their families represent accurate pictures or selective memories is impossible to ascertain. Interestingly, Entrenched bachelors acknowledge their similarities to their families, despite the negative implications that entails.

Developmental histories of Entrenched bachelors reveal that they began their adulthood with less focus and little direction. Some report feeling "lost" throughout their twenties. They had little idea what they wanted to be when they grew up, and so they were aimless. However, in their early thirties most Entrenched bachelors apply themselves adequately, so they achieve career stability. The income potential of Entrenched bachelors is about the same as that of other men, although there are probably fewer jobs with which they feel comfortable. They seek unchallenging jobs, which fit their desire to be on their own. They become janitors or delivery truck drivers, or they find ways to limit the interaction they have at their job.

One Entrenched bachelor, Ernie, reports being satisfied with teaching in the same high school classroom for the past 22 years. Although teaching is a job with high social contact, Ernie's characteristic dreariness emerges as he states, "I like the fact that I can use the exact same material in class after class without having to revise it at all. Same room, same classes, lots of free time." Like Ernie, most Entrenched bachelors do not make waves, so they settle into jobs in which they are being, at a minimum, retained and, in some cases, promoted. They go home alone immediately after their work day is over. They prefer to live alone. Interestingly, although the average income of Entrenched bachelors interviewed was about equal to that of the overall group, fewer of them owned their residences than did the rest of the men. They may avoid putting down roots.

A case example will further illustrate how one Entrenched bachelor goes about his life and will show how these bachelors are different from the other two bachelor types.

DESCRIPTIVE CASE STUDY

Eddie has lived in Chicago for all of his 43 years. Nothing physically marks him as an Entrenched bachelor. He looks fit, standing about five feet eleven inches tall; weighing 180 pounds; and sporting a tousled, thick head of sandy-blond hair. His appearance is unremarkable with the exception that he does not maintain the kind of eye contact that engages most people. Instead, he either looks away or fixes his gaze slightly askance, as if addressing a person in the unoccupied seat next to his interviewer. He is attractive at a distance, although his fleeting eye contact diminishes his appeal.

Eddie has one older sister and three younger brothers. He says that his family "cared about each other, but we never did anything as a family unit. There was a real sense that you were on your own. There was love there, but not a closeness, not a lot of togetherness. There was a respect, but a sort of 'keep your distance.' I think I wanted more, but it was an okay family." Although Eddie expresses a feeling when he says, "I think I wanted more," he cannot better articulate what he means. He also distances from his feelings by putting them in the past—even though he once wanted more, now he thinks his family is okay.

Eddie's parents were married for 47 years until his father died 3 years ago. He describes their marriage as a "true marriage, a good marriage," but also says "knowing human nature, perhaps my father cheated on her once or twice, nothing that anyone really found out about." Eddie describes himself as being similar to his father in many ways, including being "frugal and miserly." While Eddie is referring specifically to money matters, he is probably also alluding to affection and emotional warmth as well. His father was "a strong person, a loyal man who stayed with the same company for years. He was a steady person with an overriding sense of responsibility, but also a man intolerant of the things around him." Eddie believes that "my father wouldn't have been married if he was born at the time I was."

Eddie earned a bachelor's degree in history from the University of Illinois at Chicago. During college he lived at home with his parents for the first year and then shared apartments with school-mates when he could afford it, moving back into his family's home when his money ran short. Eddie volunteered to be interviewed after having read a personal ad placed in the *Chicago Tribune* asking for bachelor volunteers. Avoiding taking a stand, he shows some confused thinking when he states that he responded to the ad because "Well, I never saw an ad like that. I said, 'That should be good.' I love to put my thoughts down, though I'm not sure I have any thoughts."

At the time of the interview Eddie's living arrangements were atypical of those of most bachelors because he shared his rented apartment with a woman. Lifelong bachelors in general, and Entrenched bachelors in particular, want—even need—to live alone. In spite of sharing his apartment, however, in many ways Eddie turned out to be no exception: He was decidedly unhappy about having a roommate and had no emotional attachment to her. He asserted his independence as he was quick to point out that this woman was "just a roommate living here because she had nowhere else to go. She's been living here for two months, and I dearly wish she would move on, but I can't throw her out. She has taken up too much time currently." As Eddie talked about Ms. X (he never, in over four hours of conversation, mentioned her name), he sometimes became confused about their roles and called her his "girlfriend," but he was always clear that he wanted her to move out. Eddie was concerned that she not be present while he was being interviewed, not even in another room. He was so apprehensive, in fact, that at the last minute he rescheduled an appointment when he learned that she might be home.

Eddie allowed Ms. X to enter his life in a moment of agitated vulnerability when, literally, his defenses were down. Two years prior to our meeting, when Eddie was 41, he had an atypical period of soul searching, which led him to believe he was stagnating and he tried to set some new goals in his life. Getting a girlfriend was one of his goals. At the tail end of this period he met the woman in question in a local bar. They had a few drinks together, they talked, Eddie invited her home, they had sex, and that was the end of it. However, a few months later she came to him in search of a place to stay. "What could I do?" Eddie questioned. "I couldn't let her live on the street, so I suggested that she live here until she finds something." He was generous, but now his inability to assert himself is leaving him miserable.

He assumed that she would stay for two or three days and then move on, although they never actually discussed it. Now it was two months later. The woman was still there. Eddie found her presence to be highly intrusive. His sexual desire for her, which had always been quite emotion-free, had vanished the moment she moved in. He is no longer sexually involved with her. Simply having to coexist with her day after day arouses enough anxiety in him to destroy the concentration he needs to enjoy his sole pastime, reading. Through all this, however, he could not bring himself to broach the subject of her departure with her. This is what can happen when a person becomes too dependent on conflict avoidance as a psychological defense. Because he usually avoids dealing with others, Eddie is incapable of directly addressing problems and shows the extreme passivity in human interaction that is a hallmark of Entrenched bachelors. Like other men in this group, Eddie was pessimistic about his ability to change or improve his life. He felt so powerless to get the woman to move out that he saw no point in even making an attempt. He withdraws rather than trying to meet his own needs.

Eddie had lived with another woman once before. Notably, he could not recall the precise dates of this significant relationship, exemplifying the vagueness of Entrenched bachelors. About his prior experience with cohabitation Eddie explains:

When I was in my late twenties, I lived with Sheila for, maybe, one or two years. It was a very serious relationship. We were going to get married. We never did. It was probably my fault. She was hot for marriage. I didn't see any point in it. I guess I was kind of wishy-washy about the whole thing. I was content, happy even. Then she left me. But, heck, no use looking back and dwelling on it. I guess my heart wasn't in it.

Sex between Eddie and Sheila was "hot and heavy until we moved in together, then it trickled off to almost nothing." This is similar to what happened with Ms. X, the nameless woman who was his current roommate. Between Sheila and Ms. X there was another girlfriend, and again this sexuality pattern prevailed, prompting Eddie to joke: "Maybe if I had gotten married, I would have no sexual desire at all." He muses that "a high level of sexual satisfaction was there for a while, but then I never lived with her. If I had moved in with her, it might have reached the point where we stopped having sex. I think I would kind of be afraid of that in a marriage."

For a never-married man Eddie's initiation into sex occurred early, at age 17. However, rather than an act of assertion and confidence on his part, here he also evinced his passive approach to interpersonal contact. "It happened on a date," he said, "and it was more her doing than mine." This illustrates his lack of assertiveness in relationships and shows his abdication of responsibility, a sign of avoidance. His passivity and lack of assertiveness are also evident when he states, "I take life as it comes to me, and I'm not a threat to other people." In most respects he seems calm and content in the world he has created for himself. He describes himself as "loyal to the people I know and easygoing."

Like most Entrenched bachelors, Eddie doubts that he will ever marry. "I'm the kind of person who should not get married," he observes. Consistent with his inability to view marriage and other relationships from an emotional perspective, Eddie perceives that men marry "for social reasons, to be a regular person." He sees himself as an individualist. Thus, he chose to live with two former girlfriends rather than marry them because, as he put it, "Why bother with formality?" When asked to explain what makes a relationship serious, Eddie demonstrates his emotional detachment with his reply:

I think one thing in having a serious relationship is that it is going to continue and that you want it to continue. Probably the biggest single thing about getting serious is that this is something I don't want to stop; I don't want it to end. And when you realize that you don't want it to end, then you really are looking for what is the best for all parties concerned . . . what's best for her, what's best for you.

This is a characteristically vague response. Significantly, in answering, Eddie does not think to mention love. He continues to explain why he will probably not marry as he says: "I have a yearning for privacy, and I don't want anything to change. I have gradually evolved without marriage, and I have no interest in raising children. Maybe that's a flaw, but I think that's why a lot of people get married. I know I have no desire for children; that's for sure."

Also contributing to his evaluation that he should not get married is the fact that Eddie wants to live alone. He is not happy about having other people intrude on his personal space, and he feels threatened when they get too close. "Women need to be talked to," he explains, "and there are times when I don't want to talk to anyone." Not having to hold up his end of conversations is in his view a virtue of not being married. Lacking the interpersonal skills needed to deal directly and effectively with others, he is able to preserve his tenuous sense of self only by isolating himself from people.

Although his slavish adherence to containing his feelings and his passive avoidance of interactions with others are limiting, these defenses work for him insofar as they enable him to maintain his status quo. However, Eddie fears that maintaining his current situation is being threatened in two ways. One threat is the increasing level of discomfort he feels from sharing his apartment. The second threat comes from a possible job promotion, which would "make my job become more social. I would like to keep my outside world 'safe,' and now I am going to have to interact more with people, maybe go to meetings in Springfield, and it might require that I make some changes. . . . I want to remain 'independent,' and I'm not sure I will be able to do that if this position changes."

For six years Eddie has worked as a bookkeeper in financial records for the city of Chicago. He finds his job "satisfying and comfortable because it is not very challenging or demanding." His job appears bland and colorless, much like his apartment, which is a drab, gloomy place filled with musty air and with paint peeling or discolored everywhere. Although the furnishings were comfortable enough, little attention has been paid to decor. In his apartment, and on the job, Eddie appears content to mark time, keeping his eye on the clock, waiting for each day to end. His salary ($32,000) keeps him comfortable. The job demands no ambition and only minimal effort from Eddie, and he likes that. Had he been married, he concludes, his lack of drive would have been unacceptable to his wife. "I would have been forced to go for more money, and I would have had to hustle more. The fact that I am not married has allowed me just to settle into this position." This pattern of settling and maintaining was exemplified consistently throughout Eddie's life. Prior to his present position, Eddie had worked for an insurance company that wanted to enroll him in a fast-track training program, but he deferred, stating, "I said, forget it. I don't need it. If I had a wife," he added, "I would have had to have gone for it."

In these ways Eddie remains unmarried as a way to limit the demands and expectations that he is not sure he could manage. During the times when over 90 percent of his peers get married, Eddie has chosen to live in self-imposed solitary confinement. Aside from reading, his only pleasure is driving around in his car. He claims to have male friends, "but not that many," and he has a difficult time identifying his current male friends. His degree of isolation is such that his "best friend" lives two thousand miles away, and "I don't talk to him very much." He yearns to expel his sole woman "friend," Ms. X, from his apartment. These contradictions force Eddie to distort reality and fit it into a pattern that makes sense only to him in order to keep his thoughts clear.

Eddie would not venture a prediction about his future. He found the subject "boring." He says, "In a lot of regards I am someone who is standing still. Yet in a lot of ways I have grown, moved, and matured—I'm not the same person I was in high school, but I have never been someone to make plans or really had goals for the future." Like other Entrenched bachelors, who typically were noncommittal in their statements and outlook, Eddie seems to avoid thinking about tomorrow out of self-protection so as not to arouse anxiety based on uncertainty. When forced to consider his future, he seems a bit confused and disjointed in his response: "I can't say anything about the future. I just don't know. It is real unclear, especially if I don't get some help in figuring out how to make changes; I just don't know. I would like to change. Maybe marriage would make things better, but I'm not sure."

When asked what the worst thing is about being single, Eddie observes, "Nothing really is so bad, but sometimes I think about the future, when you are older, and I think you can suffer then. There could be a lot of loneliness in your life. If you have a spouse to grow old with, that is a wonderful thing. Living alone when you are seventy—I don't know if I will enjoy that." Though the sentiment was charged with some feeling, the voice in which it was delivered was emotionally flat. And by putting the feelings thirty years hence, Eddie also protects himself from an emotional reaction too close to home. Also, putting problems off for thirty years once again shows Eddie's commitment to the status quo and his desire for consistency. He will never marry.

UNDERSTANDING THE ENTRENCHED BACHELOR

Entrenched bachelors are the only bachelor type who with any great consistency qualify for a diagnosable psychological condition. Many, though not all, fit the criteria for the mental disorder of Schizoid Personality Disorder. In a random sample of the population at large the number of Schizoid Personality Disorders would be expected to be less than 1 percent (American Psychiatric Association, 1994). Among Entrenched bachelors, however, the percentage of Schizoid Personality Disorders is considerably higher.

What exactly is a personality disorder? Psychology recognizes that we all have certain personality traits—enduring patterns of perceiving, relating to, and thinking about the environment and oneself. Traits are exhibited in a wide range of important social and personal contexts. These traits help make us the people we are. Having certain traits alone does not lead to being diagnosed as having a personality disorder. It is only when the personality traits are *inflexible* and *maladaptive* and cause either significant functional impairment or subjective distress that they constitute personality disorders.

Beyond these general conditions that result in having a personality disorder there are specific diagnostic criteria for Schizoid Personality Disorder. These criteria include a pervasive pattern of detachment from social relationships and a restricted range of expression of emotions as indicated by not desiring or enjoying close relationships; choosing solitary activities; having little interest in sexual experiences with another person; enjoying few, if any, activities; lacking close friends or confidants other than first-degree relatives; appearing indifferent to the praise and criticism of others; and showing emotional coldness, detachment, or flattened affect (American Psychiatric Association, 1994, pp. 638–641). At times persons with Schizoid Personality Disorder may look depressed because of their emotional blandness and diminished activity level. However, when asked about their moods, these people do not report sadness or gloom; instead, they are emotionally flat. Consequently they do no not feel bad about their condition.

So if these Entrenched bachelors often have this important-sounding condition of Schizoid Personality Disorder, why aren't they in distress? An interesting paradox of this mental disorder classification is that personality disorders do not usually lead to ill feelings for the persons who have them. Since personality disorders represent chronic, long-standing, and pervasive patterns of relating, the persons so diagnosed see these patterns as "normal." Because personality traits are usually in place by adolescence or earlier and continue through most of adult life, they are so familiar to the persons exhibiting them that they usually are not recognized as problematic. People become used to a certain way of getting along and simply see it as the way things are. However, people with personality disorders can become problems for the people around them because they are so inflexible. This was the case for Ben, the 43-year-old bachelor described in Chapter 1 as having been dragged into counseling by his girlfriend, Jill. She wanted him to make room for her in his life, but he had no intention of doing so.

Because those with personality disorders are not very adaptive, their entrenched personality traits can break down under stress or develop into self-defeating cycles. For instance, a schizoid person's social withdrawal does not promote better understanding of people, which leads to the increased likelihood of his receding further from social relations. In addition, even in difficult situations the person with a personality disorder is more likely to look for the problem outside himself than turn inward to examine his contribution to the problem. This makes change even more difficult.

Because people with personality disorders do not suffer a lot, nor do they see their problems as rooted in themselves, they have little reason to change. Some personality disorders, like Antisocial or Histrionic, are particularly disruptive, and those who have such disorders may be told by others that they have to act differently. People with these personality disorders are most likely to get hassled by people at work or by significant others. However, since most Entrenched bachelors usually do not make waves at work and have few significant others, there is even less likelihood that they will be inspired (or required) to make personal changes.

People with personality disorders, although not well adjusted, are not despicable. Their ways of relating foreclose the possibility of achieving the advantages of marriage, but in many ways they are existing on a level at which they are most comfortable. If they want to change their lives, we could be available to assist them, but it is not for us to judge the appropriateness of their choices. Eddie relates with only a basic understanding of how people get along, so that even the most superficial interactions with others are potentially threatening. It might be in the best interest of someone like Eddie to have others back away from him unless he invites them close.

Eddie and other Entrenched bachelors possess a minimal conception of what it is to let another person into their lives: to communicate, share feelings, be intimate with another human being, and form a bond based on mutual interest. Such knowledge is encoded in the mind early in life as a result of children interacting with each other and, more important, sharing, observing, imitating, and learning with their parents. A child who is reared with minimal human warmth, either in an impersonal atmosphere or with cold and unaffectionate parents, will be deprived of early sensory and emotional stimulation and learn how to get along without it. Such youngsters are apt to develop an interpersonally detached and emotionally withdrawn air and have awkward relationships with others. For instance, Ernest, another Entrenched bachelor, answered the question "What would you consider your greatest achievement?" by saying, "I probably haven't had any," but then he went on to list five. What the listener is left with is a confusing and perplexing sense about Ernest.

What must not be lost in this discussion is the fact that by and large Entrenched men are satisfied with their lives. True, their lives are so narrowly defined that many potentially enriching experiences are excluded, but that is not how they see it. From where they sit, their personal style makes sense: They do not know anything else and probably do not want to. Within the safety of their own tight worlds they are content. This satisfaction that Entrenched bachelors experience draws sharp contrasts between them and the Conflicted bachelors in the following chapter.

7

CONFLICTED BACHELORS: THE PROBLEM OF AMBIVALENCE

All bachelors have strong commitments to self-determination and autonomy. Some also want to be married. Those in the third bachelor type, Conflicted bachelors, have mixed feelings about being single. These men are dissatisfied with their single status, but are reluctant to give up the independence that they imagine they would have to compromise in marriage. Conflicted bachelors are discontent with being single because they observe shortcomings when they consider their significant relationships.

Conflicted bachelors are highly aware of the advantages and disadvantages of being single. They also see advantages and disadvantages of being married. They have staked out a position in which they are psychologically invested in both the single and the married camps. As such, Conflicted bachelors are quite uncomfortable. Their opposing internal forces cause stress. Conflicted bachelors are sincere about wanting to be married, but back away from taking the plunge. They say that they are seeking to make a serious commitment to an intimate relationship, but then find reasons (excuses?) why this is not happening. Their reluctance to fully engage in one position or the other leaves them despondent.

Conflicted bachelors, probably 50 percent of all bachelors, are different from Entrenched bachelors because they are more interested in having close relationships. Entrenched bachelors are spared the angst that Conflicted bachelors feel because their desires and behaviors are consistent. Entrenched bachelors are unequivocal in valuing the individualism and autonomy that can come with being single: They do not vacillate in their appraisal like the Conflicted bachelors.

The ambivalence they feel about their marital status also differentiates Conflicted bachelors from Flexible bachelors. Confident about their choices and self-assured that they can meet their interpersonal needs when they arise, Flexible bachelors are more positive about their lifestyle. Flexible bachelors have the courage of their convictions and seem to act more on their beliefs: If a Flexible bachelor feels lonely, he gets on the phone and corrects the situation. Conflicted bachelors are more likely to be dejected and consternate about being alone. Conflicted bachelors may not lack courage in their convictions, but by comparison they can look wishy-washy because they vacillate between wanting to be married and wanting to be single. Their diminished confidence when compared to Flexible bachelors contributes to Conflicted bachelors' discomfort.

Weighing the advantages and disadvantages of being married or single is not unique to Conflicted bachelors. Certainly their Flexible and Entrenched brothers are aware of the available options. However, Conflicted bachelors dwell on whether or not their choices have been optimal. They ruminate over their situation in ways that Flexible or Entrenched bachelors never would. As Conflicted bachelors waver between their two desires, they inhibit the satisfaction they might have with their single status. They are not content with their single status, but they also have grave reservations about the alternative. Conflicted bachelors' ambivalence is palpable.

Some Conflicted bachelors spread their frustration around. Conflicted bachelors are the bachelors most likely to drive a woman crazy. As Conflicted bachelors bounce between wanting to be married and wanting to stay single, the ambivalent turnabouts they make when it comes to being married can catch their girlfriends by surprise. A Conflicted bachelor might one day say that he intends to marry and the next day be off asserting his independence. For instance, Clive relates that he bought a child's bicycle seat for himself after spending a delightful day cycling with his girlfriend and her young son. He recognizes this purchase as a symbolic act of moving closer to her, and he was seriously considering their union. However, within a week of his purchase he broke off the relationship, and within two weeks he returned the bicycle seat. He never told his girlfriend of his purchase.

Compared to the other bachelor types, Conflicted bachelors tend to have intense relationships of varied duration. Differentiating them from Entrenched bachelors is the fact that they do seek and establish romantic relationships that sometimes last for years. However, Conflicted bachelors generally lack the consistent emotional availability and steady resolve of Flexible bachelors. In their most extreme conditions Conflicted bachelors' relationships may be marked by separations, arguments, flight, and reconstruction as they oscillate between simultaneously clinging to significant others and expelling them. Noted psychologist Hans Guntrip refers to this process in its extreme as the "schizoid compromise," in which the individual "hovers between two opposite fears, the fear of isolation in independence with loss of his ego in a vacuum of experience, and the fear of bondage to, of imprisonment or absorption in the personality of whomsoever he rushes to for protection" (1969, p. 291).

On the other hand, Conflicted bachelors are the bachelor type most likely to marry. Their desires for closeness and relatedness can win out against their fears of intrusion and demandingness. They desire change because they are uncomfortable, and they see advantages in being married. In fact, because they struggle with their feelings, Conflicted bachelors who are able to resolve their ambivalence about marriage may make good husbands. If they successfully address their mixed feelings, sharing concerns rather than acting them out in non-constructive ways, Conflicted bachelors may commit with more intensity to a wife and family than do Flexible or Entrenched men who marry.

Most Conflicted bachelors establish a sense of autonomy during their mid-twenties, settling into comfortable career positions and staying there. As they grow into mid-life, however, they are less pleased with their positions and are looking to approach life differently. Conflicted bachelors usually say they desire change in their lives. Holding these Conflicted bachelors back, however, are questions about their ability to bring about improvements. To this end many Conflicted bachelors seek professional help to resolve their emotional turmoil. Three-quarters of the Conflicted bachelors interviewed had sought professional help to address their mixed experiences in relating to significant others. Most Conflicted bachelors value the consultation they receive from psychotherapists, although full resolution of their concerns takes great effort.

The discord that Conflicted bachelors face as they view marriage follows two qualitatively different experiences. One ordeal relates to those men who have feelings of insecurity and fears of competence. The other Conflicted bachelors show salient features of anger and resentment. Two case studies are offered to illustrate these experiences.

DESCRIPTIVE CASE STUDIES

Dean typifies the Conflicted bachelor who is insecure and worried about his competence. Like many Conflicted bachelors, Dean shows ineffectual and somewhat helpless characteristics, which are highlighted in his interpersonal relationships. He sees himself as hapless, sometimes coming off as a sad sack. He is not a comic character, however, because his pangs of self-doubt and personal angst are genuine. Although eager to be married, Dean lacks confidence about choosing the right woman; he states, "I want to keep my options open, so what if I get married and the next day meet someone else who looks even better?" His insecurity is especially observable in his comments about his inability to construct a happy marriage.

Dean, a 41-year-old professional, lives and works in Chicago. He is a good-looking, bearded man, although his slender, five foot eight inch frame does not make a strong impression. His slight stature is not aided by his quiet voice and nasal whine. Most of the time Dean's initial responses to questions are single words: "yes" or "no." He has to be guided into self-exploration. He appears quite ill at ease talking about himself. These attributes would not increase the listener's sympathy for his observations that the world has not been nice to him, but he is a personable individual who probably extends himself to his friends.

Dean works as a commodities trader. He says that he is doing "okay" with his income of $87,000, but "that amount isn't anything special for where I'm at." Dean describes himself as being easygoing and a "non-risk-taking individual." When asked how these aspects of his personality fit with his high-pressure occupation, he explains that there are ways to minimize risk in his profession:

> I am able to control the level of risk that I take. A lot of the guys down there in the pits are going for the big hits and are putting a lot of money on the line all the time. What I do, however, is to keep an eye on the small movements and pick up the difference between what is being sold and what is being bought. In that way I never make a lot of money on a trade, but you are never going to see me lose big either.

Dean grew up in a Chicago suburb, the only child of his Jewish parents. His parents were each married for the first time to each other, though at ages older than their cohort (his father was 41 at the time, his mother 36). His family "was very loving, with lots of attention focused on me." His parents had "a long, good marriage" until his father died five years ago. His family seemed to protect Dean from feeling too many negative feelings, and he reports a "wonderful" time growing up. Dean attended a public university in another part of the state and received a degree in business. He has spent many of his adult years "trying to recapture the happiness that I had as a child and young man. My college years were very carefree and happy. I was protected and getting away with murder—we just had fun, and had no responsibility. I never thought about growing up."

Dean marks a real turning point in his life as losing his first love at around age 27. He was devastated by the loss and feels "this could be a real cause of my not getting so involved, why I have played it safe." While they had not been engaged, Dean says, "She was a part of me. I loved her, I trusted her, and she dumped me. I was hurt, burned. It felt like a death. I think this made me think about opening up. I couldn't handle it, even though I probably wouldn't have married her anyway." The disturbance Dean felt from this experience seemed to be a residue from his family experience: He did not learn how to manage personal losses. His parents' protection left him vulnerable to the devastation he felt when his relationship ended.

But now Dean says he wants to be married. At the same time he is conflicted: He wants the freedom, flexibility, and emotional safety of being single, but is also "tired of being alone—I want a plan for the future." Dean wants to be in a partnership, but is afraid of "getting hurt, and this makes me not want to open up." He has been in several serious relationships. The ones in which he has shared his feelings have left him emotionally hurt. Like most Conflicted bachelors, Dean says he is "looking for an independent woman, a self-achiever who would not be dependent on me." Dean likes being in relationships because "I always have more fun when I'm with a woman. I like being with them and sharing things to do. We would be planning a future, and I become more alive, and we do more things together." In fact, Dean's activity level goes down when he is not involved with a woman. He relies on them to spark his interests, and they get him involved in activities. "I guess I lead a very boring life. It is very routine, and I don't like routine. I belong to a health club, but don't go too often. I also read a little, but I have been lax lately . . . not involved in too much."

Dean shows the insecure theme among some Conflicted bachelors when he is reluctant to become fully involved with a woman because he wants reassurance that the relationship will not be pulled suddenly out from under him, leaving him empty. He is insecure about knowing that a woman would stay with him, or that he could handle her leaving if (when?) they separate. "I'm not very good at seeing things that go wrong in relationships; the end sometimes comes out of the blue," he explains. His fears about personal adequacy, about not being good enough, run deep within him. Consequently he vacillates between thoroughly throwing himself into a relationship and backing away from it.

Another concern Dean has in relationships is his sense of "giving up my own identity" when involved in a serious relationship. He explains his concerns by saying:

When I am in a relationship, I do things because I want to spend more time with the person, but it tears me away from really what I want to do. I do things, and it's not necessarily because the person is pushing me—they don't demand it—but I do it because I know they want it. I do it, but it takes away from something else I want to do. I give in because I want to be nice. There is no demanding; I could do what I want to do, but I don't. And I always say the next time I have a relationship, I am going to do exactly what I want to do, but I don't. Right away I start giving in; I start changing things around. I might enjoy it at first, but maybe down the line I resent it. But then I had set precedents, and it's hard to revert. You set precedents, and you can't go back.

Dean seems unprepared to negotiate to have each person's needs met in a relationship.

Illustrating his ambivalence, Dean sees marriage as a risky business, but says that men get married for "security." He sees marriage as a way "to share a life, to have someone to love you and to whom you can reciprocate." The ability to merge into a partnership, however, is in part predicated on each person's confidence to also be a separate individual. Dean appears to be one of those people who is so threatened by being hurt that he defends against the potential pain by never getting too connected. He describes his struggle with finding a healthy balance between connecting with a women while not losing himself in the process as he states his personal reason for not having gotten married:

> I feel like, if I gave of myself in a marriage like I do in a relationship, then I would be so hurt if it ended. I feel like in the past they have all inevitably ended: I never had any relationships that really lasted. Even if I pushed these other ones to marriage, they wouldn't have lasted, so then I feel like it won't work. And I am trying to change that thinking, but it has been true in the past. . . . . If I got married, I would almost want a contract, and that shows how negative I feel about it.

Some Conflicted bachelors are also concerned with the burden of "carrying" a wife. They are anxious about attending to their partners' emotional and physical needs. Dean expresses this concern when he says, "The best part of being single is to not have to worry about other people's problems. And not worrying about somebody else's job, and her boss and her bills and her car, it's nice; it gives life a certain simplicity that is rewarding in itself."

But these advantages do not stop Dean from considering marriage. In fact, Dean was engaged at age 30. He remembers being passive in this undertaking as he reports:

> We had gone out a year already, and she wanted a commitment, and it was sort of an unofficial engagement. I still needed some more time. She had been at my parents' house and told them we were engaged. But it wasn't through my own volition. I didn't come out with it. I really did want it, but I wasn't quite ready. And then things changed. I found things wrong with her after that. I just found things wrong with her.

Dean had lived with a woman for about a month when he was 40. He describes this experience in ways similar to the way in which he described his prior engagement:

> I sort of felt like I got pushed into that one. Well, not pushed; I asked her to move in with me, and if things worked out, then we would get married. But I was more casual about it. She was very specific and forthright in saying, "Now that I am in, what are we going to do." There was nothing to do at that point because I wasn't ready. I felt the same way as her; I felt it just wasn't the right time. So things spoiled, and she moved out. There is very much a battle between me and them [his girlfriends].

Dean is right; there is a battle between him and "them," but as a Conflicted bachelor, the struggle is also inside himself.

Dean feels he has not been ready for marriage because

> I matured late, and consequently I don't understand relationships very well. You see, when I was young, I looked even younger. When I was 22, I looked 17, and it was just difficult. I wasn't dating much, although I wanted to, but it was just difficult at that time to have relationships. When I was about 27, I started to blossom more as far as my desirability to women.

Dean further describes the slow progression of his growing up by answering the question "If you look at your adult life as a trip, how would you describe your journey?" with the following metaphor:

> From high school to 25 years old I would have been backpacking throughout Europe and Indonesia and Africa. Studying and learning different cultures on the trip, staying in youth hostels, exploring, just kind of watching, I guess. It was like spending one month per place. From age 27 to 35 I moved up, got rid of my backpack, and began traveling first class by train. I was longer in each place, maybe four months. From age 35 to now [41] doing much less traveling and having much less interest in traveling alone. In fact, there is no desire to travel alone any longer, but I am staying put and living much more luxuriously.

Like many bachelors, Dean became sexually active later than would be expected. He had first intercourse when he was 26. Since that time all his relationships have involved sexual relations. Dean was uncomfortable talking about his sexuality, but did reveal that "it is usually hot and heavy at first, but doesn't really go anywhere later on." Not surprisingly, given his insecurities, Dean states that physical appearance is an important attribute in the women he dates. It appears that many Conflicted bachelors need to feel they are worthwhile because they can be with attractive women. At the same time, however, many of these men may come to resent or be threatened by their girlfriends' beauty.

As is common for never-married men in general, Dean's milestones and points of personal transition were not brought on by himself—he was reacting to things outside himself. The first transition, at age 27, was a result of his first girlfriend breaking up with him. In reaction to this event he said, "I spent a year away from here and went to Southern California. I got away and did things for myself. After a year I learned that I could be by myself, and I also learned that I wanted to be back in Chicago."

The second transition point, at age 35, was brought about by the construction company for which he sold prefabricated room additions going out of business. He was forced to find new employment and chose to move to the commodities trading floor. He is proud of this decision, stating, "It was a real risk to initiate the move to the trade commodities, and the fact that I have been able to do it makes me feel good about myself."

His phrasing of this response—that is, locating the source of his feeling good about himself in some external situation—gives more evidence about his tenuous sense of self-esteem. In addition, as insecure individuals will often do, Dean compares himself to people around him. The upshot of this evaluation is that he usually uncovers faults in himself. For instance, when the observation is made that he is making a good living, he states, "I guess it sounds like that, but there are a lot of guys down there making a whole lot more."

Part of Dean's attraction to marriage is its potential to make him feel good about himself, to feel like he "belongs" and "is like everyone else." But his internal conflict and personal insecurity interfere with his taking definitive action. He recognizes that an old pattern might doom his hopes: "I want to give in to this desire to be married, but I know that she would have to be perfect or I will start finding fault with her, and then the relationship won't last and I can't stand losing someone. I want them to reassure me that the marriage will work out. You know, if only I didn't need a woman, things would be okay."

Dean became teary-eyed when he related his desire to become more connected with a woman. He even inquired about how psychotherapy might help him change his patterns in relationships. When asked if he wanted a referral to a psychotherapist, Dean said that he had seen a psychotherapist for three sessions a few years earlier, a fact that he had withheld when asked about this earlier. His personal reticence shows itself when he states that "I guess I'll return to therapy, but it costs so much and doesn't seem to do any good anyway."

In looking to the future, Dean is typical in expressing a desire for change and in doubting that things could be improved. He imagines, "My life will probably go on the same way as it has. Unless I really give in and really want to get together with someone. I need to give in and find some happiness. There will be ups and downs, and I will go along the same way unless I make changes and get honest with myself. I still don't know what will happen."

Dean's conflicted feelings are shown in his desire to remain the way he is, yet also wanting to be married and have children. These mixed feelings, and his resistance to change, are exemplified in his comments about the couch in his apartment, when he observed that "I want to get a new one, but if I do that, go out and pick out a couch that I want for myself, I will be accepting the fact that I am a bachelor, and I don't want to be a bachelor, so I will wait for the right woman to come into my life, and I will let her pick it out with me."

Like some Conflicted bachelors, Dean feels a strong desire to have children of his own. For him this desire is stronger now than ever in his past. He says, in fact, that "at this point having children is the reason why I would get married." When asked if he took part in any activities that channeled his parenting desire into productive interaction with children, Dean fell back into his avoidant defense, stating:

Well, I thought about being a Big Brother, but I just haven't. I don't get involved. It takes a lot for me to go out and do something like that. I'll think about it, but I just really don't care to open myself up to something like that, so I don't. I know I'd probably like it a lot, and I know I'd probably get so involved in it, it would be hard to break away, and so I don't get started.

Carl, like Dean, typifies many characteristics of Conflicted bachelors. He implements the emotional defenses of avoidance, isolation, and distortion in mixed and sometimes erratic fashion. He has genuine desires to be connected to others, but pulls away from the complications that go along with emotional closeness. In contrast to Dean, for whom insecurity interferes with his getting his needs met, the main block for Carl is his anger. Carl has a broad streak of animosity, which pervades his emotional life and his relationships. He can be a bitter person. At times he sounds like he could be hostile and attack others. However, he holds his behavior in check by pulling away from stressful circumstances so that he does not act out negatively toward others. Although others might find him oppositional or negative, his benevolence is also genuine.

Carl's antipathy toward others appears to be more extreme than that of most Conflicted bachelors, but he highlights many of the core elements of Conflicted bachelors who exhibit a belligerent posture when interacting with others. These men probably appear less sympathetic than the insecure Conflicted bachelor subgroup exemplified by Dean, but they deserve equal concern because they, too, are struggling to relate to the best of their ability.

Carl is a 43-year-old high school science teacher who grew up as a middle child in his large Catholic family. He has the appearance of an athlete, carrying his slender, six-foot-three-inch frame with an air of confidence. He attended a Catholic college, returning to graduate school in his late twenties for a master's degree in chemistry.

Carl recalls his family with distressing memories of his mother verbally abusing his father and attempting to control each family member's life. He resents the kind of control his mother exercised within his family. For instance, he recalls:

Dad would never argue with my mother in front of us. She would yell at him, but he would never argue with her in front of us. I suspect he sometimes said some things at other times, but I don't think he was ever real strong about it. We used to make jokes about it. She called him a senile old fool in front of us once, and every time we were around him we'd call him a senile old fool in front of her. We'd laugh, but we kept saying that. He wasn't even allowed to use her first name in front of us. It had to be "Mother"; it couldn't be Betty. She was definitely in control, and she had no business being in control.

Carl says his mother had no business being in control because she was too demanding that everything had to be her way. She seemed to have firm expectations of what was best for everyone and then would set out to make that happen, resisting any deviation from her plan.

> Sometimes she would get it right, and certain advantages would come our way, like being pushed into the right class at school. But most of the time it was her way or no way whether she was right or not. And this was the way we all dealt with each other, too. Those conditions made me angry then and make me angry now. Like I am trying to live up to some set of rules and expectations someone else set out for me, and I hate that.

As he reflects on these early irritating events, Carl peppers his conversation with the fact that "I am working to mature beyond these old feelings of resentment," but clearly this is hard for him. Carl finds it easier to move beyond his negative feelings when he forms new friendships; he is less able to move away from them with his family. Actively avoiding extended contact with his family is his primary method to get beyond his angry feelings. Although he enjoys his siblings when they get together one on one, Carl says he will not make the thousand-mile trip home

> if any other kids are going to be there at the same time as me. You see, I like to do my own things when I want to do it. If there's two or three of us kids there, our mother will always be wanting us to do something. They'll say, "Let's go to a movie," and I'll say, "I don't want to; I just want to stay home and read a book." She'd get ornery and drive me crazy by saying, "You're being so negative." I've left the house a few times, and she would literally just drive us out of there. One time my mother tried to trick me by saying that I would be the only kid visiting, but then my brother and sister-in-law showed up, so I got on the next plane out of there.

Carl says all six children in his family are intelligent and successful. His own sense of success comes from his 22 years of teaching. His current assignment is in a large, suburban high school.

> I can't even tell you how important my teaching is to me. I feel like I really reach many of my students and show them how to reach within themselves to find excellence. Granted, I don't get to them all, no one could, but you cast a big net and catch a few. The ones who are ready come in after school and take in a lot of the wisdom that you can deliver to them. Knowing that I have had a positive impact on kids who otherwise might not have gone to college or who would have felt shitty about themselves is very important to me. I am overjoyed when former students return to visit and show what they have learned.

Carl's sense of accomplishment with his teaching is not matched in his interpersonal endeavors. He wishes that he got along better with others so that he could have more friends. He wants to have more people "who really know me." Carl seems painfully aware that his sometimes unfriendly manner prevents him from having easygoing relationships, and he wishes he got along better with others. "I used to yell at people if they cut me off on the highway. And I was angry a lot because no one would listen to my good ideas. I am less that way than I was before, but I still react to others with being pissed off. I have too many feelings of anger and resentment, which have led a lot of people to see me as arrogant."

His angry feelings can be particularly focused on women. He describes them as controlling, demanding, inflexible, and "unable to relate." While he uses these condescending terms to describe women, Carl also feels very attracted to women, even to the point of "desperately wanting" specific women at certain times in his life. Currently not dating anyone, in his past relations Carl enjoyed the

> togetherness, and the stimulation, when I was in a good relationship. The stimulation was physical, but when things were good, it was also intellectual. I like being challenged to think, and having someone to read books with and talk about shows we had watched was great. I could imagine myself marrying a very bright woman and having long, deep conversations with her. I miss that feeling of growing together and coming to greater ideas because you develop your thoughts in conjunction with another person over a long period of time. That is why I would like to get married because I think there

are great opportunities to really become synchronized with another person.

Carl would like to be married because he enjoys so many aspects of his serious relationships with women. However, Carl also uses several poignant words—trapped, forced, controlled—when talking about what he did not like in his relations with women. These experiences keep him from actively pursuing a spouse. Intimacy with women, and interactions with most people for that matter, threatens Carl's tight hold on his anger. "Women get to me, and that has been a problem. I have a sort of poverty mentality. With some women I feel like I'm not worth much and I have to convince them that I am worth something. I was in awe of them. I would see a pretty girl and say 'I want one of those.' They were pretty, cute, small, and seemed strong, and that scared me."

Carl says that his poor opinion of women was engendered within the all-boy schools that he attended while growing up. Graduating from high school, he continued as a member of the Catholic order of Franciscan Brothers and received his teaching certificate. He taught with the Franciscan Brothers, an order of men who practice celibacy, until age 28, when he left for public life. During his years with the Franciscan Brothers Carl felt

> discordant with my environment. I loved teaching high school, but it just wasn't working beyond that. They had ideas about how to live and how a person should feel, but there was no sense of doing it. I was angry and overate to deal with the anger. I got up to 300 pounds, and then I knew I had to get away from them, so I got a science foundation grant and went back to college for my master's and on to public school.

Carl knows the exact date of his sexual initiation, saying, "This is important to me because I was so much older than my peers." He was 32 years old.

> I lost my cherry late. I never did lose it in that [first] relationship. It went on about eight months, but it was neurotic as hell. You know, it was like pure grasping. We didn't know ourselves very well; it seems like we just felt like we had to be with another person, so we clung to each other. She went off to some guy in California, and then

my next relationship I swore I was going to get laid this time, you know, and I did.

Since that time he has slept with ten women. He has become less sexually active since turning 40. "I still like to be held by a woman, but I think my sexual slowdown has come about for two reasons. First, I feel uncomfortable with feeling encroached upon; I like my space. Second, I am less driven to get something for myself because I am more at peace with myself." Carl has achieved his peace

> in part through psychotherapy, or whatever it is that I am doing with my therapist. I have gone for a few years now, and I feel like I have a better sense of who I am, and who I am in relation to what I want from the world. Knowing myself better, I feel like I can bottle up my anger and put it off in a corner of my mind, so that it doesn't ooze out and get all over everything I touch. I keep it off to the side through meditation and reflection.

Maintaining his sense of peace is threatened by getting too involved with a woman. Isolation is one way Carl controls his feelings. However, relationships are important, and he says that sometimes "I feel really lonely." Day-to-day encounters are infrequent for Carl:

> But that is okay. I more highly value deep, intense, short-lived encounters with extended contacts. I have friends, but not real close friends who would just stop by. I can feel crowded by friends. They can infringe on me. I like to sleep alone and have my own space. I spend my summers seeing friends. We hike and get really intensely interested in each other. Then we spend months apart, with almost no contact.

Though very involved with his students in school, Carl does not have an interest in having children of his own. He compares having children to "having pets; they are all-consuming. They take too much care." Though he expresses a real desire to get married, Carl feels that he would probably not do so as long as he holds his current job because "I get real involved with my students, and I get my needs for personal development met through their successes."

Carl relates that he would like to make major changes in his future and explore a different lifestyle, maybe going back to school to be a therapist or retreating into a monastic life. However, he laughs as he relates that "my current job, with its high [$46,000] salary, has me just as trapped as if I had a wife and family."

UNDERSTANDING THE CONFLICTED BACHELOR

Dean and Carl are examples of Conflicted bachelors, men who value individualism and self-reliance, but who also want to be connected with women through marriage. As these two men demonstrate, Conflicted bachelors tend to not be very happy people. They have a hard time blending their personal allegiance to both single and married values, so that Conflicted bachelors can be emotionally torn. Because they rely on social and emotional distancing to maintain their well-being, their opinions of themselves fluctuate depending on how they are getting along with others. Conflicted bachelors can be unsure of themselves.

Conflicted bachelors can also seem like enigmas to others. On the one hand they are reserved and detached, but then they throw themselves into activities. They work on being self-sufficient, but they get lonely and want to connect with others. Dean, for example, asks a woman to move in with him, but then turns around and gets her to leave. All the while he is reluctant to invest himself in a new couch for fear that his next girlfriend will not like it. Carl goes out of his way to help his students and relishes their personal growth, but he finds not being able to find his TV remote control too much of a hassle when he has friends over, so he spends most nights alone.

Both Dean and Carl demonstrate personal views of the world that impinge on their ability to reach their personal goals. For instance, Dean's expectation that people will keep track of his mistakes leaves him unsure of himself when he acts definitively or expresses his opinion. Carl's expectation that all women are controlling and demanding is also at odds with reality, but still curtails his efforts to share himself with them.

Although similar in many ways, two noteworthy subgroups of Conflicted bachelors exist based on their reasons for not marrying. Some Conflicted bachelors are insecure; others are angry. For these two subgroups the seeds of their ambivalence seem to have been sown in the families in which they grew up. Dean, and other insecure bachelors, reports growing up in pleasurable and comfortable families. However, the idea that commitment to a woman arouses fears of making a major uncorrectable mistake seems to be consistent with the way they grew up. Whether based on reality or simply their own perceptions, these bachelors feel that their families can be picky and judgmental. Acceptance of outsiders was low among their families. Some men in this group talk of having a potential wife who had some quality that made her unacceptable to his family. Fears of making a major mistake were sometimes related to the limited people skills these men felt they observed and learned growing up.

Conversely Conflicted bachelors with angry undertones, as exemplified by Carl, report growing up in emotionally hurtful home environments. Some men report personally "hellish" family experiences, while others report less stressful, though still "contentious," families. As much as they wanted to be with others, these men feared, on conscious and unconscious levels, that relationships of their own would resurrect their painful experiences from childhood. Growing up with many resentful and angry feelings, these bachelors work hard to control their internal turbulence. Connecting with others threatens this control. To their credit these men work hard to manage their feelings without damaging others. Harm is being done to themselves, however, because their need for tight control requires an attentiveness that prohibits unrestricted emotional interchanges.

Conflicted bachelors are less self-sufficient and more self-doubting than are Flexible bachelors. Conflicted bachelors are more interested and involved with women than are Entrenched bachelors, but their inconsistent interactions can lead to similar awkward social interchanges. In contrast to these other two bachelor types, Conflicted bachelors lament not having things the way they want them. They wait for the "right woman" to come along, but then find reasons to keep her at arm's length. They wish for more male friends, but do not do much about bringing this about either.

Paradoxically at the same time as their ambivalence leads Conflicted bachelors to have strained relationships, their mixed feelings probably make Conflicted bachelors the most likely bachelor type to marry. Their dissatisfaction with being single, and the fact that at least part of them wants to be married, leaves them open to changes in their marital status. In addition, as they get older, Conflicted bachelors' interest in being married seems to increase.

Do they marry, remain ambivalent, or resolve their conflicted feelings in other ways? Preliminary answers to these questions are offered in the next chapter, which reports on tracking bachelors' life experiences over a four-year period.

8

BACHELORS FOUR YEARS LATER

Dean got married! This Conflicted bachelor, moved to tears because he was so unhappy at age 41, when contacted four years after his initial interviews, reports:

> I wanted to get married, and I found the right girl to do it. She was 38 years old and never married. She had good values and comes from a good family. She is a good person and very pretty. I was tired of dating women. We met in June, got engaged in August, and were married in November. I was surprised about how easy it was to propose to her; I had never proposed to anyone. I was ready, and she was ready, too.

Consistent with his ambivalent personality, however, Dean also reports:

> I'm not real happy about being married. The adjustment has been real difficult. There is a control issue there: She is very strong about having her own way. At first I was happy, but at about the end of the first year she began to take my freedom away. She wants to know where I am going, and now I can't do anything on my own. She has some strong ideas about what a husband should be, and she doesn't back down from them.

Dean is pleased that the loneliness he used to feel is gone, but he is disappointed by the loss of freedom he feels. He is surprised by this feeling because he and his wife

> talked about my need for independence before I agreed to get married, and now she has changed the agreements. It's not like we had a prenuptial agreement, but we sat down, and I told her what was important to me, and she reneged on this. We've already gone to a marriage therapist once, but we didn't go back. She didn't like the therapist, and I didn't say anything. Maybe we will go again.

Other, less dramatic events have also changed Dean's life between the ages of 41 and 45. For instance, although still working as a commodities trader, Dean has doubled his salary to about $175,000 per year. He has moved out of the city to a home in an upscale Chicago suburb. He had not followed through on his plan to see a psychotherapist on his own, but he feels he is eating better and working out more, so overall he reports being healthier. He is concerned that the problems in his marriage will interfere with his desire to have children because he reports that "we will not have children until we work things out." In spite of the shortcomings he observes, Dean is committed to his marriage, stating, "There have been lots of times since I got married that, if we were just dating, I would have called it quits. But because we are married, I have hung in there. I feel challenged to work things out. In some ways I am pleased with myself for hanging in there through the hard times to try and work it out."

Although several aspects of his life changed, Dean's inner experience has not been transformed by getting married. He does not appear to have resolved his ambivalence: He still maintains one foot in both the single and the married camps. He continues to be dissatisfied with how he gets along with his significant other, remaining stressed about relating because he feels constricted by his wife. Although he blames the shortcomings of his marriage on his demanding wife, we have to question how much of his angst is generated from within himself because he reports having felt very similarly with another girlfriend whom he had dated prior to meeting his wife. He also reports that he resists his wife's demands because "it's really hard for me to have anybody telling me what to do. It's not even like I would want to do a lot of things with the guys, but it is hard for me to be dictated to."

BACHELORS ARE CONSISTENT

The major life changes that Dean has undertaken are unusual among middle-aged bachelors. Sameness and psychological inertness are more the norm. This observation is based on follow-up interviews conducted with the bachelors four years after their initial participation in the study that underlies this book (Waehler, 1992). This kind of longitudinal examination is often lacking in psychology. The renewed contacts with these bachelors allow them to be seen more as moving pictures than snapshots.

What we see in looking at this group of never-married men is that Dean is the exception among the bachelors interviewed because he reports major life changes during these four years of his life. Most (over 80%) of the bachelors followed over these years simply continued what they were doing during their first interviews. Both the psychological and the behavioral trends over the four years were continuations of their prior activities. For instance, the men who were dating someone before tended to be dating someone now. If their pattern had been to date a woman for a year or two at a time, then that was also the case during this new time frame. If they reported having no significant relationships with women during the earlier interaction, these bachelors reported similar scenarios. These repeated practices sustain the bachelors in the level of satisfaction they had first reported. For instance, Flexible bachelors, gratified with their prior activity, continued to be pleased with their lives four years later. Similarly the dissatisfaction reported by Conflicted bachelors during their first contact continues among the men in this group.

Although it makes sense that the satisfied Flexible and Entrenched bachelors would wish to maintain their previous undertakings, the disconsolate Conflicted bachelors settled for the ease of repetition rather than attempting mid-course adjustments. Conflicted bachelors' entropy does not reflect their satisfaction with the status quo. On the contrary the ease and comfort of familiarity, even when the experiences being repeated were by their own admission less than ideal, appeared to be what motivates these men. Most Conflicted bachelors, dissatisfied with their limited relatedness with others in the first interviews, reported the same discontent four years later. David, for instance, was displeased with the fact that his girlfriend of 15 years had discontinued their sex life, but he continued to see her while maintaining his mandated celibacy four years later.

These observations display how deep the core personality traits run. The core bachelor personality characteristics, and how they were acted on to categorize each man as Flexible, Entrenched, or Conflicted, continued over this new period of time also. Their initial personality types continue to correlate with how they feel about their current lives.

The extended contact with these bachelors leads us to a not-al-together-unexpected conclusion: The vast majority of bachelors hardly change a bit. Most had said they planned to marry, but only one in ten had. Remarkably even their expectation that they would eventually marry had not been modified: Only one bachelor who thought he would eventually marry had changed his mind about this prospect. All the bachelors who thought they would not marry stuck to this prediction.

Is this stagnation what we would expect of men during their forties? On the contrary the 40–50 age range, termed the "Mid-life Transition" by social scientists, marks for most men the most dramatic psychological change since the onset of puberty. For instance, Daniel Levinson and his colleagues note that during the Mid-life Transition the life structure comes into question:

> It becomes important to ask: "What have I done with my life? What do I really get from and give to my wife, children, friends, work, community—and self?" A man's yearning for a life in which his actual desires, values, talents and aspirations can be expressed comes into question at this age. . . . For the great majority of men this is a period of great struggle within the self and with the external world. . . . They question nearly every aspect of their lives and feel that they cannot go on as before. (Levinson, Darrow, Klein, Levinson, & McKee, 1978, p. 60)

Shifts and changes can be dramatic—changing one's career, getting married, or seeking divorce—or subtle—altering ones attitudes toward family and friends, thinking differently about the future. But in either condition the reappraisal, exploration, and testing of choices are discernable.

Fewer than one in five bachelors contacted reported experiences that would serve as markers of a Mid-life Transition. Some individuals had undertaken personal life changes like moving from one house to another, but questioning the meaning, value, and direction of one's life—the developmental task observed by others—was not approached by these men. Because lifelong bachelors tend to limit their involvement with others—they may avoid dealing with the normal demands of life. As a result their personal development may be marked more by consistency than by adjustment.

Some bachelors, in fact, are resolute about how consistent their lives have been. Along these lines Eddie, the Entrenched bachelor who was miserable because he had a roommate in his dank apartment, reports:

> My life is the same. I still see the same people and drive down the same streets, come home to the same apartment. Really nothing has changed. I did take that job that puts me in charge of some other people. For the most part that is okay because I enjoy the flexibility, and I enjoy the increase in pay. But except for that, nothing else has happened to me.

One aspect of Eddie's life shows incredible consistency: Once again he has a live-in, non-lover, female houseguest. This time "we were sort of going out, dating. Then about a year ago she lost her apartment and moved in here. A few months after that her brother moved in with us, too." Similar to our first contact, Eddie is unhappy with his living arrangements: "I feel encroached upon, and it feels pretty intrusive." Also consistent for Eddie is his passive acceptance of his living conditions. He relates, "I don't really like it, but I don't feel like I can do anything about it. I guess I am sort of getting used to it."

"Nothing comes to my head when I think about what might be different in my life now" is Ernest's response to questions during our renewed contact four years after the first. This 54-year-old Entrenched bachelor, who gets moved to different parts of the country about every year and a half for his civil engineering job, states, "I've been doing exactly the same things these last few years as I've always done." Ernest shows his passive approach to life as he vaguely wonders, "Maybe I should change things. Maybe I shouldn't get so involved in my work. In the last four years I got involved in one relationship, but it just kind of drifted apart. It was kind of fun, but we had our own interests, so we just drifted apart. I don't see too many people, or keep up with people."

Fred, the employee assistance consultant who described himself as "straight, single, and solvent," shows his same optimistic outlook as he observes:

> There have been a lot of bad changes in my profession, so I feel very lucky to be working, and even luckier that I have increased my salary [to $200,000]. The only thing that has changed in the last four years for me is that I moved from one office to one down the hall, and, in fact, I moved my home from one condominium to the one right next door. Wow, that is an interesting parallel.

Fred had a serious relationship, which lasted two years. He enjoyed it, but "she likes living in the suburbs, and I like living in the city." Although they had many hobbies, interests, and values in common, he supposes that "living arrangements came between us, and so did our 14-year age difference." But the major problem, which he did not imagine would resolve itself, was this:

> We kind of had a terrible sex life. She was kind of emotionally closed off, and sexually un-innovative. She is gifted with a good mind, and a good sense of humor, and she is a great tennis player. But she was not very giving sexually. And she also was incapable of talking about it. Sure, it is hard to talk about sex, but she couldn't even agree that we needed to talk about it. So that became the shoals upon which our ship foundered. What scared me was that she was not very free, and I couldn't imagine such a situation getting anything but worse. And as much as I like her, and we had an otherwise great relationship—we were, and still are, great friends—I wish we could have overcome that. I am sorry that we could not overcome the hang-ups.

Fred, showing his casual, flexible approach to relationships, continues to imagine that "I would be happy to be married. I am not against marriage, but I am very used to being single, so getting married seems a bit less likely for me."

Carl, the high school science teacher who was often angry at his world, says that during the last four years "I got a dog and changed my address so I am about three blocks from my school. Now I can get up late and just walk over." But he also states, "Everything about me is about the same." He has not been dating anyone, but contemplates this in his future because "I think getting my dog may help me change who I am. She is the first thing I have let in my life for a long time. It is nice having someone like me like that, and it causes me to pay attention to someone else, and it isn't so bad. She makes me feel more open to having someone around." Carl keeps up with his meditation and reading so that "I feel less need to defend myself, and I find it easier to get along." Although he continues to enjoy his students' development, he looks forward to an early retirement in seven years.

Frank, the personable mathematics professor from Wisconsin, spent a year in Japan on a Fulbright scholarship. He relates his experience as "a real adventure."

> More than before I recognize that there are so many things that a person really can't influence much and can't control. I would describe myself as a person who enjoys being in control and is in control. I am that way, but I am more able to recognize that the best thing to do is to just expect that things are going to happen and go from there. Look forward. I don't moan and groan to myself as much as before about things. I think I am more accepting than I was before.

Frank's year of living in a different culture led him to appreciate that

> the Buddhist precept that "suffering is the result of desire" is something that really rings true. This relates to my single status. I feel like I am less desirous than I may have been before. I had never been real driven, but now I feel even more willing to let things go the way they will—which is interesting in some ways because I also feel like I am more assertive and outgoing regarding relationships with women than I was before. I am more looking for ways to get to know people than before.

Frank has been initiating more dating with women because "I feel quite comfortable with myself. In the past I used to feel like I was 'pitching' myself to women, and if they didn't want me, then there was something wrong with me, but now I see it as much less psychologically risky. I am less concerned about being under inspection."

Frank also relates:

> Having been in your study also made me think about my life and my actions. I sat back and thought about the work I do, which I love, but also that if I would like to be close to other people, which I do

enjoy, I have to take more initiative and not necessarily do anything different, but take more charge of what I do. Not that I have to do anything that much different, but that I can do *more* of the kinds of reaching out that I was already doing. In the past I feel like I got carried along by circumstances. Living a good life where my job could take up all the hours of my day if I let it, I am now taking more time to meet the many interesting people in the world.

Frank reports dating to be "comfortable and enjoyable," whether or not it leads to anything serious. Most serious among his relationships over the last four years was a woman in Chicago whom he dated for several months after being introduced to her by an old college friend. "We were pretty involved, and I thought it might be going somewhere, but she broke it off. I think because the distance [three hours] was too much for her to negotiate. We had a lot of laughs and a lot of good times, but she just wanted it to be finished." When Frank and this woman broke up, "we just kind of went our ways. Nothing bad; I would still consider her a friend."

When personal intimacy develops with his dates, so usually do sexual relations. Frank continues to enjoy healthy sexuality with most of the women with whom he becomes involved. Similar to four years ago, Frank says he is ready to marry and have children and continues to expect this to happen sometime in the future. His increased steps toward assertiveness probably bring him closer to this possibility, although the calculating, emotionally reserved way with which he continues to go about his relationships might mitigate against it.

BACHELORS WHO DO CHANGE

The bachelors who changed during the time frame—three who married and one who finished graduate school and started a new profession in another part of the country—are the exceptions. However, they are also predictable exceptions. After all, based on census data, we would anticipate that about 1 in 6 bachelors will marry between the ages of 40 to 45, and 1 in 20 bachelors will marry between the ages of 45 and 50. In addition to Dean, the bachelors who married were Felix and Derrick.

Felix, the manager of his family's electronics business in rural Ohio, married the woman with whom he had been living when he participated in the first set of interviews. Together they have a daughter. In strong contrast to Dean, although consistent with his more resourceful personality, Felix is thrilled about these turns of events:

> I'm happier than I have ever been. Having a wife and daughter has simply made my world more delightful. You have emotions which you have never had before. I am glad to have them and feel that I would have missed out on something really important if I had not felt these things. The love you have for a child is something that you can never feel in another area.

In an interesting maneuver, which depicts his passive style, Felix relates that he seemed to back into marriage: "We had been living together for a while, and then we decided to get pregnant, and that was the deciding factor in us getting married. We now have a two-year-old daughter. We didn't really care about marriage, but did want to have a child, and when we were pregnant, that kind of made marriage the right move, too."

Consistent with his characterization as a Flexible bachelor, Felix is happy and relating positively. He believes he was single

> not because of any flaw, or personal problem or belief system, but in part because I was dealing with a very limited pool here in this rural section of Ohio. But my situation changed when my wife moved to this area and we were able to get together. I know it sounds kind of cliché, but I think I was just waiting for the right person or the right opportunity.

Felix's career has stayed about the same in spite of his marriage, "although having a daughter makes you use your time more wisely." Felix is pleased with the fact that having a family of his own has made him closer to his younger brother and his family.

Derrick, a Conflicted bachelor with insecure features, is the third man from the original study who married since the first interviews. Now 51, he was married two years ago to a woman ten years his junior. Derrick's feelings about marriage fall somewhere between those of Dean and Felix as he reports, "Marriage, for a person my age, is kind of an adjustment, but when all is said and done, I enjoy it. There are difficulties, but we stick together and do things together. Through it all we stick together." When pressed for details about the adjustments he has made, Derrick relates:

I had never experienced someone sort of moving into my life and rearranging things. She has a passion for decorating, and I would come in and say, "Where the hell is everything? What have you done here?" But after a while I have gotten used to the arrangement. And now she is more used to me, too, so she lets me know further in advance when things are going to be changing. There is more negotiating now.

Derrick reports that prior to getting married he was fired from a community college teaching position:

And I was traumatized. The other members of the faculty were very petty, hassling me all the time. I think they were threatened that I was having some success with some of the students. I knew I had to go when they were complaining that I mumbled too much in front of my classes. I was on unemployment for eight months after that. Now I work as a computer programmer, and I will make over $30,000 per year for the first time in my life.

Exhibiting his personal insecurities and the tenuousness of his self-esteem, Derrick says that he and his wife "bonded a great deal during my unpleasant experience at the college. I was at a loss as to what to do, and she helped me get through it with my sanity. So I wasn't getting any younger, and there didn't seem like any reason not to get married."

With only minimal reservation Derrick states that he is a good husband. He feels that he is less anxious and more confident than he used to be. He reflects that going through his own five-year psychotherapy from ages 43 to 48

was very important for my being able to be a good husband. I did a lot of self-examination and gained a real identity for myself. My therapist would ask me quite often "Who are you?" And at first I couldn't answer that without a lot of tension. I didn't know myself too well, and I needed to be kicked to make some progress. I think I also needed some guidance with my feelings. I needed a vocabulary for my feelings.

Derrick continues to "check in" with his counselor on a periodic basis "in order to get a lot of things off my chest."

Derrick appreciates the companionship, camaraderie, and support that he feels with his wife. Together they have been able to buy a house, but more than that, he feels secure in having someone who "is a friend when I need one and bolsters me when I am down."

These three men who married do not follow the traditional stereotype that bachelors, if they do marry, will choose pert young women half their age. Their mates were not calculated attempts to recapture their youth or desperate attempts to escape loneliness. Instead, they seemed to be reasoned choices to spend time with women with similar values and interests.

MAINTAINING THE STATUS QUO

One hypothesis that can be drawn from this longitudinal investigation is that Mid-life Transition may be facilitated by commitment to a partner or an attempt to establish a family. Having a spouse (or ex-spouse) or children may serve as a catalyst to the mid-life experience by forcing transitional markers on the individual. Bachelors may insulate themselves from the overlapping involvement with family members and other precipitants of a mid-life crisis (e.g., dealing with children moving into adolescence, observing a spouse's personal development, meeting the changing demands of a partner), so that the transition may be bypassed. Similar to the clam that needs a grain of sand from which to start the pearl's growth, these men may not be involving themselves enough with others to force confrontation with life's demands.

For some people desires for change come from within. For others these desires result from external stimuli. The men in this study seemed to experience little internal angst, so they simply maintained their status quo. For some people participation in a study such as this might have served as an external impetus for change. After all, each participant had received 20 or so pages of written feedback from the initial bachelor study. This feedback was a summary of what is detailed more fully in this book. Some men had an initial reaction to reading about the objective appraisal of their lifestyles, which could have startled them into making life changes, but most reported being nonplussed by it. Even the ones who had an initial reaction returned quickly to their prior patterns. Calvin, a 47-year-old high school teacher from Indiana, whose rock climbing and tennis take up most of his free time, reports the strongest reaction as he relates:

Seeing the results of your study, a study I was part of, made me really think about my life and my undertakings. I had always thought of myself as a happy person, who was pretty comfortable, but [your results] made me see that I was more dissatisfied than maybe I had imagined. Initially I was a bit miffed, but I think I realized that I miss having important relationships. To some extent I think you helped me reflect on my life, although I'm not sure what the bottom line effects have been.

Calvin thinks that reviewing the research led him to seek out intimate relationships for himself. To this end he had two serious relationships during the four years between interviews. One was with a 40-year-old woman with whom Calvin felt "more relaxed than I maybe ever have with a woman. But the timing was all wrong, as she was heading back to graduate school and didn't want to make time for a relationship. She was the one who pulled back from that relationship."

The other relationship, with a 32-year-old mother of two children, Calvin describes as "crazy":

She kind of bounced my head around for three months. We were friends, then we'd get sexual, and then she would want more of a relationship. I would have to explain that wasn't going to happen, and then she would say that was okay, then we'd get close again, then distant again. Finally she said that she was going back to her old boyfriend, a guy she had always complained to me about. I saw a therapist about this whole matter because I was really shaking my head wondering what was going on.

Calvin feels his therapist helped him enormously because "I needed to sort through this whole crazy event. I think I came to accept myself better through sorting that out." However, overall Calvin reports:

Everything is really the same for me. I'm still teaching, and I'm still enjoying it. I'm not necessarily looking for anything to change. I am going to finally finish my master's degree in a couple months, and I might look to make a change then, but I'm happy with my time in school and my time off—although I still wish I had a female partner in my life.

During the last four years several additional important events had also changed in Calvin's life. A roommate from college died at age 47, and his mother died two years ago. With regard to the former event Calvin says, "that made me consider my own mortality." However, Calvin characteristically avoids deep feelings about the latter event as he states, "It wasn't such a big deal because I feel like I had lost her a long time ago. She no longer recognized me when I would visit her in the nursing home, so her actual passing wasn't a big deal."

Calvin still imagines, and hopes, that he will get married, although he admits:

> I think I am getting more picky in my old age if that is possible. I recognize that I have a lot to offer, and now I am thinking that I would like my partner to have a lot to offer to me. I also think I recognize now that something magic is not going to happen in terms of finding the perfect person, but I am willing to compromise some independence to get together with the right woman.

It appears that Mid-life Transitions might be less prominent for those who have chosen individual paths for themselves and are without spouses or children. The continuity maintained by bachelors may also be predicated on their core personality characteristics of avoidance, isolation of affect, and distortion. Their hesitance to get involved, make demands, or assert their needs; their contained, repressed emotions, which limit their involvement with others; and their idiosyncratic style of relating may work together to insulate them from Mid-life Transitions. Bachelors may sidestep what is a painful experience for some people. However, to view this passage only as negative overlooks the fact that Mid-life Transitions promote growth in many people. A mid-life crisis can fortuitously trigger a psychological renaissance. Mid-life could be a particularly productive time for those bachelors who are displeased with their situations. Bachelors need to recognize that they have several options available to them, and that exploring these options, whether it leads to change or recommitment to the status quo, can be rewarding.

9

OPTIONS AND CHOICES FOR BACHELORS

One of the surprises for some of us as we reach adulthood is that we are still works in progress. Describing bachelors may make them seem stagnant, as if they are carved in stone, like sculptures on exhibition at an art gallery. However, the bachelor personality is not necessarily fixed and intractable. It is probably better to think of the bachelor descriptions like frames in a cinematic movie: Each is an episode in an unfolding process. As conveyed in realistic films, certain personality characteristics remain the same, but other qualities and behaviors change as a result of external forces or conscious decisions to be different. Movie characters have continuity, but the next plot twist offers novel possibilities. If this was not true, why would an unfolding story be so captivating?

This chapter invites each bachelor to step back from himself and contemplate the options and choices available. Self-examination can be empowering, sanctioning positive changes that are highly favorable and welcome. However, sometimes when we step back to objectively review our lives, it is difficult to suspend judgment while scrutinizing alternatives. We can become agitated; we too quickly criticize rather than explore. One of my fears in writing this book is that too often we associate investigating with judging. Throughout my descriptions of bachelors I have not intended to be critical; after all, I am a bachelor myself.

MY PERSONAL JOURNEY

At the time of this writing I am a 39-year-old, never-married man. Although not officially meeting the criteria of being 40 years old and never-married, the general bachelor personality characteristics fit me. In particular, I am fiercely independent and very committed to self-determination. Self-reliance is my primary mode of getting through trying times. I have always had a rugged admiration for individualism; many times I have learned things on my own when I might have been better off consulting with someone else. For instance, as a teenager I wanted to learn to sail, so I borrowed a "How to" book and a sailboat and floated around until I figured out how to catch the wind. It worked, but this approach missed the finer points, which can best be learned from a knowledgeable mentor, and I did not experience the joy that comes with shared recreation.

Although throughout my adulthood I have enjoyed several serious relationships with wonderful women, it is important to me that no one describes me as dependent. Like other bachelors, my first inclination when I feel vulnerable is to distance myself from those feelings. There are advantages and disadvantages to looking at problems dispassionately and overcoming them through independent hard work.

A humorous example of how deep my independent streak runs happened a few years ago when I was assembling a ping-pong table in my basement. After I single-handedly wrestled the bulky box into my house, I read the instructions (unlike the masculine stereotype). I grudgingly noted the directive: "For this part of the assembly, you will need two people, one positioned at each side of the table, to lift it onto the bracket." I scoffed at this and reasoned that I could get down on my hands and knees, maneuver the table onto my back, and, crawling along the floor with the table resting on my back, grab the bracket with my hands and place the table where it belonged. As I read ahead in the directions to know what assembly would be required next, I was again miffed to see repeated, "Two people are required for this portion of the assembly." I took this second warning as a personal challenge and proceeded with my plan.

The first time I tried to muscle the 60-pound table up on my back I lost my balance. Pushed down under the weight of the table

I was pinned to my basement floor. Unhurt, though extremely uncomfortable and self-conscious, I began to laugh as I pictured the headline: "Psychology Professor Found Trapped Under Own Ping-Pong Table." I laughed harder when I thought of the TV commercial with the older woman crying out, "I've fallen and I can't get up." Tears ran down my face from laughing, but I crawled out from under the table and put the table together on the third try. I gained extra satisfaction at being able to do this on my own. Not waiting until the next day to call a friend to help put the table together is the bachelor part of me; wanting the table (after all, ping-pong cannot be played alone) is the Flexible part of me.

As the story exemplifies, accomplishing tasks on my own has been a trademark for most of my life. But over the years I have learned that looking at life's emotional facets is also important. I override my natural tendencies and instead celebrate my feelings and constructively draw others close to me for guidance, support, and nurturing. In these ways I am working on being more produc- tively *inter*dependent. Because I have been able to expand these qualities, I best fit into the Flexible bachelor category (even though my name does not start with an "F"). Relating to others and flexibly including them in my plans does not diminish my independence and ability to accomplish things on my own. I have benefitted from the wise consult of others. For instance, it was at the encouragement of a girlfriend that I returned to graduate school at age 27.

My significant relationships during adulthood have usually lasted a year or two (one for six years), and each involved lots of close sharing, caring, and mutual satisfaction. Most of the women with whom I have been involved have had fantastic potential as marriage partners, and we tended to get along really well. My friends (and even some of my old girlfriends) continue to shake their heads when they consider the relationships from which I have walked away. However, in ways that have become increasingly clear to me as I have studied bachelors, I just was not psychologi- cally ready to marry.

For instance, during my first year in my graduate program I met, became friends with, and then wooed a delightful, witty, and charming woman about four years my junior. Within a few months of dating seriously, getting married became a topic of conversation. The first time we talked about spending our lives together I wept like a baby: I was quite overcome with the joy this prospect brought me. I felt like I had arrived at a wonderful destination, and I was delighted by the prospect of spending my life with Mary. We had fun together, had similar goals and values, and seemed to complement each other in ways that would make us very happy.

However, within a few months we became less close, and although at the time I could not recognize it, the bachelor personality traits described here held us back from merging into a real partnership. I spent more time on my studies and less time with her. I took fewer risks in talking about my feelings or my likes and dislikes. In short I isolated by withdrawing into myself. It got so bad that when Mary began to talk about our difficulties, I would fall asleep or be unable to think straight. By the end of a year Mary and I drifted into our own worlds independent from one another until we mutually decided our relationship was over.

When I later spoke with Mary, she told me the guy she dated after she and I broke up nicknamed me "Mr. Missed-his-chance." I jokingly corrected his observation, suggesting that I preferred to be called "*Dr.* Missed-his-chance." My comeback to Mary speaks to one of the primary reasons why Mary and I did not remain together. I recognize now that I wanted to complete my doctorate degree. I felt this would be more difficult if I was married. In addition, because Mary was so easygoing, I feared that she would disturb my focus and lower my dedication to work.

What I know now is that I should have been more vocal about sharing my aspirations and discussing my uneasiness with her casualness. Instead, I kept my concerns to myself and jettisoned her. Looking back, I wonder if I could have reached my goals if I had married. It could be argued that I could have achieved more. I'm not sure. Gaining my professional degree was especially important to me because my father had not done so for himself. My father, an accomplished accountant and teacher, twice completed all the courses required for his doctorate, but never successfully finished his dissertation. Finishing my Ph.D. was something I did on some level for both of us.

My unconscious fear was that Mary would pull me away from my mission, and I dealt with these feelings by getting rid of her. However, I did not totally withdraw from gaining care, love, and companionship: Throughout the rest of my graduate-school years, I dated Jessica. My relationship with Jessica was different from that with Mary because for the first four or five years we were together we did not talk about marriage. The fact that she had two children of her own and was older than me helped keep the discussion of marriage on a back burner. Together Jessica and I shared many warm and wonderful moments, as well as deep and important aspects of our lives. For years we had many of the components of a successful marriage.

However, holding us back was my emotional guardedness with her: I rarely spoke openly of my feelings for her; instead, I hoped she knew how much I cared about her by my actions. We were mutually committed to one another, but maintained a degree of psychological independence. This emotional distance led us to never really consider marriage. While I know that I could not have achieved as much as I did without Jessica's support, not being married allowed me to maintain the illusion that I was doing it on my own. I am eternally grateful for the support that she gave me to help me achieve my degree and grow as a person.

Another source of support throughout my graduate studies was personal psychotherapy. At first I entered psychotherapy because it was recommended as part of our training to be psychologists. However, I quickly recognized that I had a lot of personal turmoil inside me, which I needed to encounter and work through. I knew that this could best be done within the understanding, non-judgmental atmosphere that therapy affords. I was in therapy for almost four years. Prior to therapy I showed more of the confused, insecure characteristics that exemplify Conflicted bachelors. In therapy I gained more of the confidence, positive self-regard, emotional facility, and social acumen that mark Flexible bachelors. Though the self-confrontation in therapy was not always pleasant, it was important to my development: I had a lot of old baggage that I needed to drag out, consider, get angry about, deal with, and put behind me. Sometimes I have been quite angry at the world, most of the time turning the anger back inward at myself, so that I feel annoyed and exasperated.

Although these experiences still creep into my life, I have learned to differentiate the negative feelings that were justified from those that were irrationally determined from prior disappointments. I knew that psychotherapy was having a positive impact on my development when I first recognized that I consistently misspelled the word *marriage*, more often making it look like *mirage* (which I guess is what it seemed like to me). Being able to laugh at myself during and after the incident with the ping-pong table is another outcome of my psychotherapy; prior to therapy I might have been quite upset by my initial ineptitude. Feeling fully prepared to enter into a full, committed relationship when that prospect comes along is another outcome of my own psychotherapy.

Psychotherapy also helped me review my observations about how people interact. These patterns were ones I had experienced and observed during my formative years. My childhood was very positive, but my family recalls me as a child spending many hours off by myself—fishing, exploring, or reading. My two older sisters and I, although now close, grew up independently from one another, into our own activities. I learned how to get along on my own, and others left me alone.

Probably most influential, however, was the turmoil of my parents' divorce during my teenage years. Divorce per se does not push children toward or away from marriage, but how the divorce is handled within the family has significant impact. In my family it was not handled well. My parents began to separate when I was 11 years old and did not complete the process for seven years. During these years my parents reached few amicable agreements. Mean things were said. Cold messages were delivered. No reliable family core was available to me. Characteristically we all drifted independently, each licking our own wounds. I withdrew into myself and work. I gained a sense of my competence from part-time, after-school jobs, which I began at age 13. Various jobs throughout my teenage years gave me a sense of personal worth, but were also detrimental to certain parts of my growth: They kept me away from healthy interaction with other kids.

The one special place where I enjoyed continued involvement with people my own age was a coed Lutheran camp in New Hampshire. The affectionate togetherness that I experienced with my same-age friends, the substantial projects we completed together, and the long nights around campfires discussing important life issues were of inestimable value to me. I stayed on in several leadership positions for years and maintain my involvement to this day. Camp was an essential opportunity for me to learn the joy of interacting with peers in both constructive and recreational activities. Without the many years of all-season activities, letter writing, and visits with camp friends, I doubt that I ever would have gained a sense of myself as a valuable and worthwhile person. With those people I learned lessons about mutuality and love that were not available elsewhere.

Like other Flexible bachelors, I like to be connected with others. Right now I meet many of my needs to be connected with others through my work. Being a professor, researcher, part-time therapist, and author gives me the opportunity to become significantly involved in many lives. I take full advantage of these opportunities, finding them quite gratifying. Right now I work more hours than would be conducive to maintaining a marriage, but I feel like I am ready to trade these hours in for the right woman. One requisite, of course, would be that she would have to honor my commitment to invest myself in my career. I can be a social person working to connect with people I find valuable. However, I also value my alone time, and at times I still feel that some people are an intrusion into my life. Being aware of this attitude helps me keep it in rational perspective: For instance, joining someone for breakfast does not mean that I cannot get a good day's work done.

I have learned how to share my feelings and opinions in an equitable fashion. Where I used to prefer to get others to talk about themselves, I am now more willing to share parts of myself. I do not know if I will stay a bachelor, as I now feel that I have matured psychologically to the point where I want more mutuality in my life. Years ago I joked with people that the logical order for constructing relationships was to first successfully grow plants, then have pets, move on to raise children, and then take on the challenge of a spouse. This progression accentuated the demands I saw in having a spouse, which seemed more difficult than the love and care that can be so freely expressed to children. As my friends have pointed out, I got a cat last year—who knows what challenge is next.

BACHELOR CHOICES

On occasion I am asked how my bachelor status influences my review of singles' experiences. When I began my investigation, I hoped that bachelors would turn out to be the best, brightest, and finest individuals around. I wanted the American ideal of the independent, self-reliant man to be confirmed when held up to scientific scrutiny. Acknowledging this prejudice, and holding it in check, I got closer to scientific objectivity. At the same time I believe my personal status assists me to relate to these men: I know firsthand the advantages and shortcomings, challenges and opportunities available to bachelors.

All people are faced with choices about how they relate with others and whether or not they marry. Relating with others can be considered in terms of isolating oneself by maintaining rigid independence and staunch self-reliance or connecting with others by striving for fuller relationships marked by emotional and social attachment. Therefore, the four bachelor choices can be seen as follows:

	Marital Status	
Relationship Quality	*Single*	*Married*
Isolated	Isolated & Single	Isolated & Married
Connected	Connected & Single	Connected & Married

The option of being single or married is listed second because being single or married is the subordinate activity. Some people get married, but never reach for high quality in that relationship. On the other hand some single people go out of their way to achieve connectedness with people important to them. Marriage does not in and of itself ensure that people will do what it takes to fully commit to another person. Therefore, people's marital status should not automatically earn them respect or ill repute. More important is what they carry in their hearts and accomplish with their lives.

Being single and being married are both legitimate and viable lifestyles. People who do not support this observation narrowly assume that good relationships are contingent on marriage. It is true that the reliable companionship that is promised in marriage can promote trust, love, commitment, and security; intimacy and shared experiences can flourish; reliable emotional support can prosper; and raising children can be passionately explored. These possibilities may be more difficult for single people. But marriage does not guarantee reaching these goals. And these days marriage may not be necessary to attain these goals. Some men become worse partners after they marry: They view their wives as the "old ball and chain," so that marriage limits rather than liberates them.

Quite frankly not everyone should be married. Mature single-hood is the optimal lifestyle for some people—but not the most popular. Throughout history marriage has been seen as more desirable than being single. Singlehood, however, is gaining in respectability and popularity. People are recognizing that the op-portunities of relationships—really knowing another person, pro-moting both personal and mutual interests, creating reliable interdependence, and championing each other's dignity and self-worth—are not the exclusive domain of marriage. Within the relationship game there are a lot of players and a lot of spectators: The players include people who are married *and* single, and the spectators also include people who are married *and* single. Mar-riage, with its social pronouncement of commitment and legal recognition of mutual interest, may assist people to figure out what their roles are when they are on the relationship playing field. However, as many people have disappointingly found out, marriage does not *in and of itself* get people to pick up the ball and run with it. Full commitment to get personally involved in a healthy rela-tionship takes place on an internal level.

Because of the secondary importance of marriage or singleness, the focus here is on the choice between being isolated and being connected. Psychological studies support the theory that people are stronger if joined in healthy relationships with others, so the latter choice is preferable. Almost every person is enhanced when people strive for full relationships. Possibilities are maximized when peo-ple reach for a healthy blend of independence and self-reliance, while also realizing full relationships. Bachelors do not have to turn themselves inside out in order to merge with others. However, moving away from extreme independence and unproductive self-reliance gives them more potential to relate energetically with others.

Connecting with others may not be preferred by all bachelors. In particular, Entrenched bachelors, who are content with their limited relatedness, are least likely to want to change their relation-ships. Independence may be the best choice if arrived at after having considered one's personality and alternative ways of relat-ing. Personal choices are not positive if they represent a retreat out of fear and anxiety. But reasoned choices that do not infringe on the rights of others are to be honored. Some men will do best to choose self-containment. They can live what they feel without making excuses. They ought to be independent and fully enjoy doing things on their own.

But, Entrenched bachelors notwithstanding, the majority of bachelors want fuller relationships. They also acknowledge that it is a true challenge. Positive relating, marked by productive interdependence and mutual sharing, does not come easily to most bachelors. Sustained mutuality in a relationship requires their concerted personal effort. But before bachelors throw in the towel, many can take solace in the fact that Flexible bachelors already relate positively and productively. These men balance their desire for independence and self-reliance with their ability to rely on others. Flexible bachelors reap rich rewards for their efforts—they are quite successful and pleased with their lives. And before we give up on bachelors in general, we ought to note that interdependence and mutuality come easily to few people—single or married, female or male. With a little work most people can make their relationships more constructive. The key word here is *work*: Healthy relationships require energy and effort.

However, the good news is that the work required for healthy relationships often involves simply modifying or increasing activities bachelors already know how to do. Foreign techniques are not required. For bachelors, with their high commitment to individualism and self-reliance and their tendencies to avoid, isolate, and distort, the move toward more interdependence involves challenging well-practiced patterns of living. But the *tasks* are not impossible. In fact, they can be exhilarating. Transforming these tasks from all-or-nothing, win-lose propositions to a process of making efforts in specific areas can help make them more approachable. And since working toward productive relationships is the best game in town, why not throw yourself into it fully?

ENHANCING RELATIONSHIPS

Actions bachelors can undertake to be fully involved in promoting positive relationships include these:

- Know yourself.
- Value emotionality.
- Be courageous.
- Be honest.

- Be present.
- Trust the right woman.
- Practice interdependence.

The first activity essential to sustaining mature, conscious relationships is *knowing yourself*. Can you easily state what brings you joy? What makes you feel fully alive, loved, challenged, supported, or intrigued? Without knowledge about ourselves—our drives, preferences, goals, expectations, dreams, and motivations—how can we join with someone else and have him or her know us? Too often we expect magic in relationships. The supernatural intervention that we hope for is that others will know what we want. We hope they will meet our needs, even when we do not know what these needs are and do not speak about them. The reality is that waiting for divine connectedness to fall into our laps leads consistently to disappointment.

Bachelors tend to view circumstances in simple and economical terms. Overlooking details and avoiding complexity argue against bachelors being naturally introspective people. In addition, being single supports these tendencies by insulating bachelors from people who would observe and comment on their lives. But introspection and self-knowledge are skills that can be learned and enhanced. Engaging in self-exploration offers hope for actively influencing our present circumstances and creating a future based on intention rather than fate.

Several tools can assist a bachelor to know himself better. A good place to start is by reviewing the psychological material regarding core personality characteristics and bachelors' views of marriage in this book. Working to classify the type of bachelor you are—Flexible, Entrenched, or Conflicted—will also help you get to know yourself better. Some men will feel like they bridge the gap between two bachelor types, but strict classification is not the goal here; self-exploration is. Trying to identify your bachelor type can act as a checklist with which to review your personal undertakings. Openly considering the best and worst parts of being single for you, the best and worst parts of being married for you, and so on will help you clarify your values.

Another resource available is a book written by Harville Hendrix, *Keeping the Love You Find: A Guide for Singles*. This easy-to-read book specifies activities to promote personal knowledge in order to improve loving relationships. Dr. Hendrix writes informatively about how our past relationships influence our current undertakings and has filled the book with practical exercises. Other books about psychology and relationships can also help you better come to know yourself. Several possible sources are listed in the "Further Readings" section. In addition to suggesting these materials, I invite you to engage in your own search of your local library or bookstore.

You can move beyond the printed page for tools to know yourself better such as attend lectures, rent audiotapes, take classes, participate in workshops, attend retreats, join groups, and talk with friends. In the interpersonal realm self-knowledge is enhanced by observing how you interact with others. Ask yourself "Why" questions: "Why did I say that?" "Why did I expect her to react in that way?" "Why am I comfortable in this situation?" "Why am I avoiding this task?" Most questions we ask on a daily basis are of the "How," "When," and "What" varieties. "Why" questions lend themselves to fascinating discoveries about ourselves.

Self-knowledge is enhanced when others join the process. Therefore, engage in discussions with valued friends about how you get along in the world. These can be informal conversations or more intentional discussions if you tell friends that you want to know more about how you come across. In addition to these informal resources, individual or group psychotherapy offers an opportunity for professional, concentrated personal scrutiny. More will be said about this opportunity in Chapter 11, but suffice it to say that for the motivated person psychotherapy can be unparalleled in helping to identify our true desires, acknowledge our inner strengths, confront our demons, and address directly the things that impede us from reaching our full potential.

Think of self-exploration as an adventure: The journey within oneself can be the most exciting trip of all. Spend some time and money on this adventure the same as you would on any other great pilgrimage—you are worth it. Consider the quest to know yourself better as a fun excursion rather than a goal to be reached arduously. However, despite the intrigue and available resources, bachelors often shy away from this enterprise because the process involves scrutinizing their emotional lives.

Because bachelors back away from emotional situations and approach them dispassionately, they will need to give special attention to this second activity essential to healthy relationships:

Value emotionality. Bachelors do not tend to prize, empower, and celebrate their feelings. Instead, they shy away from them. Bachelors' relationships, along with those of many married men, improve when they increase the value they place on their emotions.

Starting very early in their lives, our societal norm is to teach boys to repress their emotional inclinations. This leads to emotional ignorance. Males are rewarded more for thinking, judging, and doing. When boys do have feelings, they are often asked, "What are you going to do about it?" In this way they learn that feelings are legitimate only for what action they promote—and then this action is where their attention is directed. Rather than sustaining their awareness of and comfort with emotions, boys are encouraged to act quickly in response to their sensations and put these behind them. When boys move past their feelings, they are reinforced by the connection they feel with other males. During the prepubescent years exaggerated emotional repression becomes a way for boys to increase their identity as separate from girls, who are more associated with the emotional aspects of life. Although no one big event strips men in our society of the ability to value feelings, the thousands of momentary learning experiences throughout their early lives lead many men to be uncomfortable with and to depreciate emotions.

Bachelors seem to have learned these lessons especially well. They tend to be emotionally guarded people. At times bachelors may look like they have no feelings. Certainly bachelors are unlikely to have rich and vivid emotional lives. Because mutual companionship is based on sentient ties, bachelors' emotional detachment challenges their potential in relationships. Some bachelors (most likely the Entrenched bachelors) may have a biological basis for their low level of emotional arousal, and little can be done to change that. However, the good news is that those emotional patterns that result from acquired, or learned, experiences can be *unlearned*.

When we consider that men's discomfort with and avoidance of emotions are similar to other learned anxieties, like other phobias, we gain much from what the psychological literature says about getting rid of specific fears. A treatment proven effective with phobias is called gradual exposure with habituation. The task is less complicated than its name: One must gradually become familiar with the disquieting experience through exposure. Increased familiarity takes place gradually, and a person is able to progressively increase his or her involvement because initially high anxiety lessens with prolonged involvement with the stressful situation. Eventually the person feels comfortable with the circumstances that used to be managed through avoidance.

Bachelors can learn about emotions by paying attention to their own feelings and those of others. Highlight the feelings you experience in day-to-day activities; do not overlook any. Ask "What am I feeling now?" and work to clarify the experience. If the emotions feel too strong or are unclear, do not back too far away from the feelings, but instead try to clarify them. In this way the range of comfortable emotions will be expanded. Increasing your involvement with your emotional life at a comfortable, but sustained, pace will help you manage the anxiety that accompanies this new endeavor. We grow when we do not give in to our first inclination to retreat. As we experience more personal comfort with feelings, anxiety and confusion dissipate.

One potential problem in implementing this plan is that men often have a limited vocabulary for feelings. As Derrick put it, "Until I was in psychotherapy for a while I thought there were two types of emotional states: no feelings or being angry. One of the best things I did in treatment was to get a list of feeling words from my therapist. There were names for feelings that I had heard before, but I never really gave them much consideration." Like Derrick, many men imagine that the only feeling they are capable of is anger. This helps explain why they approach their emotional lives with such trepidation. Anger is particularly frightening to men because they have been taught to act on their feelings. Anger is threatening because men are afraid they will become destructive and lash out in response to their irritation. However, as they repress their acrimony, all feelings get buried.

Two aspects of anger that reinforce men's emotional repression are often overlooked. First, contrary to many of the messages we receive as both children and adults, it is okay to be angry. This can be a novel observation for many individuals, so let's repeat it: It is okay to be angry. Under no circumstances is it okay to act destructively on angry feelings, but this does not preclude allowing ourselves to *be* angry.

Consider one of our most popular American folk heroes: George Bailey, as portrayed by Jimmy Stewart in *It's a Wonderful Life*. When you look closely at this beloved character, the hero of the Bailey Savings and Loan is one angry guy. He kicks his car door; hollers at bank presidents; yells at his future wife, calling his town a "two-bit dirt rag" from which he cannot wait to escape; and violently shakes his Uncle Billy, calling him a "crazy old fool." But we love George Bailey. We overlook (or perhaps even celebrate) his anger for two reasons: He has the right to be indignant, and he channels his anger into constructive undertakings.

Twelve Angry Men, another classic movie, shows a dozen embittered men hell-bent on throwing a kid in jail. However, they come to their senses and do the right thing in spite of themselves because they eventually subdue raw emotion with reason. These men show how impulsive action on initial feelings can be harmful. But the character portrayed by Henry Fonda shows how anger can be channeled constructively; after all, the movie is about 12 angry men, not 11 angry men and Caspar Milquetoast. The difference between Fonda's character and the others is that Fonda's character uses his anger to empower himself to face the other men. The movie illustrates a constructive process, showing how coming to know the source(s) of our anger can lead us to understand it rather than act on it. The process of acknowledging and working with our anger, rather than trying to bury it within ourselves, helps us avoid unwittingly harming others. For many men permitting themselves to be angry is a key that unlocks their entire emotional life.

A second overlooked aspect of anger also shows how angry feelings can be an avenue to access an expanded emotional life: Anger is usually a secondary feeling. That is, anger usually masks other sensations. We get angry because we are lost, frightened, depressed, lonely, confused, fearful, anxious, helpless, embarrassed, hurt, or experiencing some other feeling. However, too often we do not get in touch with these other feelings because we are so busy trying to squelch our anger. We end up shutting everything else down, too.

Therefore, when you ask yourself, "What am I feeling right now?" and the answer is "Angry!" ask yourself, "And what *else* am I feeling?" If you find yourself groping for words to understand your feelings, consult a thesaurus. Another option is to convey your experiences to someone else who can help you clarify your feelings. This can be the person to whom you feel closest or someone less central to your life. He or she does need to be someone you trust and respect. Work with this person to get to the heart of your emotions. Awareness of feelings is a sensual experience, which can overflow into other interesting areas, like sexuality. Talking about feelings can be quite arousing. Men who expand their emotional lives will probably find that heightened sexual interest and awareness also follow.

These undertakings lead us into uncharted murky waters. Entering unfamiliar territory takes courage. With this in mind the third action to enhance relationships is *being courageous.*

Bachelors tend to be constricted and cautious, which inhibits positive emotional relationships. Therefore, bachelors must think about being courageous. The courage required for good relationships is not the attitude toward risk taking needed to jump out of a plane, run into a burning building, or wrestle grizzlies with a knife clenched between your teeth. Instead, relationships require the courage to say how you feel and act on your convictions. Living what you feel makes you a hero. Relationships flourish when people reveal themselves to those who are important to them. It is not enough to *consider* a kind act or a pleasant experience. You also need to *live* these feelings with others. Courage in relationships comes when you think that "it would be nice if I . . . " *and* you *do* it! Valor comes from trusting in yourself and acting on what is in your heart. Too often bachelors get caught up in their pensive, passive approach to others, so they end up wishing they had undertaken some act when it is too late and the opportunity has been lost.

The most important advice that I repeat to the passive part of me is "Don't be a coward." I keep in mind Michelle Pfeiffer's statement in *The Fabulous Baker Boys*. As she strikes out at her bachelor lover who has run from her attempts at closeness, she yells: "You are worse than a loser; you are a coward!"

An example of a man's failure to expand beyond his comfort is sensitively shown in the 1993 Italian movie *The Bachelor*. A physician retreats from his personal and professional life. He mutes his tender feelings for a beautiful woman, pushes aside her advances, and avoids making an important decision to buy his own clinic. The doctor deals with these opportunities by stepping back: He observes life from a safe distance. However, by passively holding his commitments at bay, he ensures that his dreams will not come true. When he finally realizes that he wants the woman, she is no longer available to him. Similarly when he wants the clinic, it has been bought by someone else. This portrayal is cheerless because the bachelor is successful in his fight against a full, rich life. The opportunities were available. Lacking courage, however, he allowed them to pass him by and ends up with a safe, solitary, muted existence.

Courageous acts can be simple: buying her flowers for no particular reason, kissing her and telling her you love her at some unpredictable moment, reaching to hold her hand at the movies, or initiating a discussion that you allowed to lapse. These are common examples. We each know what our limits have been. Courageous acts make us vulnerable because we push past our usual mode of functioning and take a risk that may bring us closer to our partner.

Bachelors tend to be inhibited and have a hard time asserting themselves. Their first inclination is to hold back. At the heart of their inhibition seems to be indifference or ignorance about challenging themselves. However, fear of failure is also present in many men. What bachelors (and lots of other people for that matter) need to learn is that good relationships have lots of room for forgiveness. People in good relationships give each other points for trying. That is, they recognize that mistakes happen and value those who make a good-faith effort at closeness. As in tossing horseshoes and hand grenades, in good relationships you get points for coming near the mark, even if you miss the target. Waiting to celebrate only perfect scores leaves people sorely disappointed. And then they are surprised when their partners stop trying. The challenge is to create a relationship in which you are both safe to take risks in an atmosphere of respect and kindness.

When can you practice being courageous? There are plenty of low-level challenges that test our mettle every day: Ask the boss for a raise, order some unaccustomed item from a menu, negotiate the price of a new car, go camping in an unfamiliar location, take personal responsibility for a mistake, attend a social event alone, or ask someone out on a date. All these examples require that we buck up our self-esteem and take risks. More formidable challenges come from attempts to fully embrace intimate, adult relationships: Revealing a personal fear to a loved one, sharing a lifelong goal with a colleague, telling your father that you love him, and sharing what you relish about your lover are tasks often more easily avoided than approached. Some of these everyday challenges even make wrestling the bear attractive. Sincere ventures into long-term, intimate, sharing, and committed relationships are the modern-day dragons that we men *can* slay.

A fourth way of being that promotes healthy relationships is to *be honest*. This seems like a simple act, which is easy to accomplish. But too often being honest is seen as the passive, negative process of simply not lying. Bachelors have no difficulty complying with this dictum; avoidance comes easy to them. However, being honest in relationships includes taking the initiative to make sure that your feelings and opinions are known. Being honest is being forthcoming. This is a new idea for many bachelors, who feel that exposing emotions is best handled by women. However, when both partners offer opinions, observations, and feelings, the relationship's potential is doubled.

Sometimes a man finds it difficult to be honest about his feelings and wants because to do so feels aggressive. Either he does not want to impose himself on a woman, or by revealing himself, he fears that a woman will use that knowledge against him. Either he aggresses against her or she against him. Both are intolerable. These difficulties can be modified by increased skill at negotiation. Negotiation in relationships allows each person to stand up for his or her rights without stepping on the other's. This assertion without dominance does not come easily to bachelors, but can be learned. *Your Perfect Right* by Robert Alberti and Michael Emmons describes steps that help people understand what is involved in being assertive. Also, assertiveness training workshops and classes are offered by many schools, mental health agencies, and counselors.

Being honest requires communicating clearly, not a bachelor strength. They tend to think idiosyncratically, which makes it difficult for them to join in full dialogue with others. Therefore, bachelors need to make extra effort if they want to have an understanding relationship. They need to take the time to work at being understood, to talk and listen actively. Being a good listener is not the passive process of remaining silent in order to give the talker center stage. An active listener concentrates on what the talker is saying and periodically reflects back what he hears in order to check out its accuracy. Communication is a two-way process in which the talker *and* the listener are both working to clarify and understand the messages. Both remain open to having their reflected statements adjusted because both participants are searching for accuracy, not competing for correctness.

A fifth action bachelors can undertake to promote healthy relationships is to *be fully present when relating*. Being fully present means using your five senses to concentrate on the other person. You do not want to compromise important discussions with distractions like reading your mail or walking from room to room. Instead, being fully present can be enhanced if you look at her when she speaks, listen actively to what she says, and sit close enough so that you are fully engaged with one another. Taste, touch, and smell come most obviously into play when we are fully present during sexual experiences, but verbal interactions can be enhanced by not compromising these senses by placing a bowl of potato chips between you when you are talking. When you are fully present, you see who she is at the very moment of your interaction; you are not visualizing what she was saying last week or trying to remind her of her plans for tomorrow. The full energy of the interaction is heightened by keeping it in the here and now.

Women value partners who are fully present. They find the mutuality invigorating, leading them to feel completely alive and able to grow. Being fully present is an important gift that we can give to the people for whom we care. Men also find it exhilarating, and maybe this is why we sometimes avoid it. Remaining in the here and now can elevate and intensify feelings, something that is difficult for bachelors. Muting, mollifying, and tempering feelings are more typical.

You can move toward being more fully present in simple ways: Turn off the television when you are having a conversation; do not invite a bunch of friends along on a dinner out together; put away your work papers when she tells you about her day; remember her particular brand of an item when you pick something up for her; turn off the radio when you make love; and concentrate on what she says when she talks.

Bachelors sometimes avoid behaviors that move them closer to women because they feel a danger of being engulfed or swallowed up. By taking these steps, bachelors worry that they will lose their autonomy. These fears can be allayed by negotiating precise times when the relationship will come first. One method that many couples find helpful is to hold onto two specific half-hour time blocks during the week (or whatever time feels like a bit more than the couple is having at this moment) when everything else is set aside so that they can devote their full attention to each other. Although setting up an appointment can feel artificial, it protects time to attend exclusively to one another. A specific starting time for this interaction makes it more likely to happen; a stopping time agreed to in advance can help the interaction end on a high note. Having no boundaries prevents beginning and allows negative endings when one person is forced to cut off the interaction because of other life demands.

An alternative consideration in analyzing why bachelors are not fully present is that the fears that a partner wants to limit their independence is real. There are some women who do want to dominate their partners. Therefore, another important aspect of relating fully is to find and *trust the right woman*.

There are two requirements to trust: Join with a good woman, and then maintain faith in her, even in the face of adversity. Lots of people who search for the perfect mate end up empty and alone. What they do not recognize is that establishing a high-quality relationship with sustaining power is based on what you build together, not just on what you both independently bring to the relationship. Instead of approaching relationships in a manner similar to planning and establishing a successful career, some people approach affiliations as if they are playing the lottery: They hope that luck will lead them to great fortune. This makes happiness a real long shot. Rather than seeking that one elusive winning jackpot of a person, people would be more successful if they sought a partner with whom they can grow together: Someone who is willing to share the work and joy of relating.

The characteristics desired in a lover are quite individual, but if you are seeking a partner, you would do well to consider a woman who is not expecting magical connections, but instead wants to work at making a good relationship. Look for someone who gives you points for trying—who appreciates that we all fall short, so the only way to keep going is to give each other credit for making a good-faith effort. Also a key for successful collaboration is establishing the degree to which you can be assertive with her. Knowing that you can stand up for yourself without being bullied by her—or, conversely, harming her—will allow you to engage more fully in the relationship. Success is predicated on being with an individual with whom you can maintain a positive responsiveness so that you do not aggressively defend your position or meekly acquiesce. At all times reciprocating her positive actions with your own hard work and appreciation will enhance your relationship.

The second part of trusting the right woman is for you to remain convinced that she deserves your dedicated attention, even at those times when you question your commitment to the relationship. Once you know that she can affirm your independent ways, do not pull the rug out from under your relationship if she asks you to be more involved. Keep your perspective. For example, if she wants to have input into how you are dealing with a situation at work, it does not mean she wants to strip you of your autonomy. When she asks you to commit to specific meeting times, this does not mean that you are no longer independent. Bachelors have the potential to misperceive these minor, legitimate requests, to distort them into major impositions. Remember your partner's positive qualities during these uncomfortable times while you determine whether her actions ask you to be compliant and dependent or simply to function as a couple. Keep in mind that relationships are predicated not on total dependence or independence, but instead on interdependence.

If positive relationships are your goal, it is worthwhile to *practice interdependence* actively. Interdependence is the range of behaviors between the extreme poles of subservience and isolation. Interdependence represents a state in which people rely on and are influenced by one another, but still maintain their individuality by flexibly being independent some of the time, dependent at other times. Rather than considering that you must be at the exact middle point of perfect interdependence at all times, set it up so that you can move adaptively in one direction *and* the other. This approach is more forgiving and therefore easier to maintain. Bachelors can fear getting stuck at the subservient end of the spectrum. In response, they flee to independence. Because dependence is so uncomfortable, they cling to independence until it calcifies into isolation. People who increase the flexibility with which they move along this spectrum have the most potential for productive relatedness.

Bachelors can practice versatility—being dependent in one activity, independent in another. You do not have to wait for that special woman to come along in order to practice being interdependent and to strengthen your relationship skills. Bachelors have

friends and colleagues in a variety of settings who provide opportunities for establishing mutual interests, sharing confidences, and
exploring productive relatedness. For instance, rather than taking
on a work project alone, invite the collaboration of a colleague.
Although the task may not be perfect, the process can be enlightening. The best people with whom to further develop interdependence will be bright, reflective, independent thinkers who are able
to flexibly entertain alternatives and fully engage life. Seeking those
people out in a variety of settings and practicing getting along with
them will enhance the bachelor's potential in more intimate relationships. Men who fear that being dependent during one interaction means that they will never be independent again will have the
most trouble moving toward interdependence. They need to confront and overcome their irrational concerns if they are to relate
successfully. Real strength comes when we can allow ourselves to
depend on others.

The common message for bachelors in these actions is to not
limit yourself. Reflect on your options, and whatever you choose,
pursue it with full energy. Passion, commitment, and resolve make
accomplishments more possible. Some men are reluctant to look
at their lives because they worry that they will only see what is
missing. Initially that may be true, but recognize that discomfort
can also be constructive. As men we are taught to be goal-oriented
problem solvers: to identify a problem, devise a plan to overcome
it, implement the design, complete the task, and move on to
something else. This paradigm can be problematic when tasks do
not require an immediate solution, but rather need attention to a
process, like relating to people or simply living.

Another deterrent is that many men approach new ideas like
high mountains that have to be climbed in one afternoon, barefoot,
alone, and without a map. With this perspective it figures that they
do not start the journey enthusiastically. Remember that journeys
do not need to be hurried, equipment is available, companions are
willing, and maps and guidebooks can be consulted.

Some of the bachelors I have spent many hours with have not
yet learned this lesson. Edgar, whose apartment walls are barren
after seven years, could go to an art store and pick out some
inexpensive posters and pictures to bring more spirit into his home.
Or, for even less commitment, he could find a library that loans art
to its members. If he does not trust his own taste, he can take

someone with him. Dick could get out of his self-declared five-year rut of dating his girlfriend every Saturday evening for dinner, a movie, and their same, tedious sex, only to go home for the night and then return to spend the next day with her. He need not start with a wild sexual fantasy, but he could see his girlfriend on a different night of the week, meet her in a novel location, or spend the entire night with her.

Chris, an overland truck driver for nine years, laments that he wants to write a book on how to drive. "So many cars, especially as they are getting smaller, are so dangerous. Mine would be a book to help car drivers negotiate the highway because they are so much at risk. I've seen too many accidents." But Chris has not started his book. Instead of tackling an entire book, Chris might write a letter to the editor, an article, or a short manual. In this way he might find someone with similar interests to share the task, or he might be directed toward additional resources and interested people. Lifestyle changes can be approached in deliberate, measured terms so that challenges are accepted as manageable rather than feared as onerous.

Life is not to be conquered, but to be lived, a moment at a time. It is important to start. When you stand still, you will not trip and fall, but neither will you ever see the myriad of sights and sounds offered by the journey.

10

BACHELORS AS DATES AND MATES

A woman involved with a middle-aged, never-married man is confronted by a curious situation. On the one hand here is a man who brings less "baggage" with him to a new relationship: He does not have an ex-wife to contend with, nor does he have children whom he must support financially and with whom she must build relationships. On the other hand, however, if she is interested in marriage, she ought to know that based on both census data and human nature, a bachelor is likely to remain single forever.

The United States Bureau of the Census (1993) data from the 1980s and early 1990s predict that a man who has not married by the time he is 40 years old has about a 1 in 6 likelihood of ever getting married; for a man who is age 45 and has never been married, the likelihood goes down to 1 in 20. These figures, of course, talk about trends among large numbers of people and, as such, do not predict what any single person will do. Each man makes the personal choice for himself about getting married; after all, someone is the 1 in 6 or the 1 in 20.[1]

Human nature provides the basis for a hypothesis regarding the infrequency of marriage among age 40-plus bachelors. Human beings are creatures of habit and are likely to repeat past experiences rather than embark on personal transformations. Although personal change is always possible, past performance is usually the best predictor of future behavior.

In addition, we are reinforced by our environment. That is, when we act in certain idiosyncratic ways, people around us notice and react to these habits. People respond to us "as if" we are certain types of persons. After a while they expect us to act in certain ways. People are most comfortable when we act in ways that are consistent with what they anticipate; consistency makes the world more predictable. Consistency makes life more manageable. The roles we take on and for which we are reinforced help to simplify our complex world.

Roles, once set in motion, can easily become self-fulfilling. For instance, parents watch their toddler son pick up a tennis racquet and swing at imaginary balls. They begin to tell their friends that "he is quite athletic and is going to be a tennis player." Soon they are buying him little tennis shoes. As he grows older, they enroll him in tennis lessons and rent tennis training videos, and, lo and behold, he plays a lot of tennis and gets pretty good at it. Later the parents proclaim, "We knew when you were one year old that you'd be a tennis player, and we were right!" This pattern comes full circle when the son now defines himself in part as a tennis player.

I have heard people who are trying to change through psychotherapy report, "My friends tell me that I am acting out of character by. . . . " This observation is often unnerving because the new behaviors are thought of as improvements by the client exercising them, and the comment "You are acting out of character" is usually meant (or at least perceived) as a put-down. The best response to "You are acting out of character" when trying to make personal changes is "Thank you for noticing that I am being more resourceful."

Single men, as they grow through their twenties and thirties, dating but not marrying, can be responded to *as if* they are never going to get married. They begin to be defined by observations such as "He lets the good ones get away," or "He is the self-reliant one," or "He'll never give up his freedom." Whether or not these statements are correct, other people's behaviors begin to reflect their remarks: Friends may be less likely to fix him up, or, when he is dating someone, may be more reluctant to get to know his girlfriend because they expect her to be a short-term involvement. In return, we often act according to what other people expect. The bachelor may stop asking friends to introduce him to women, he may begin to look at each woman as a brief involvement, or he may not introduce a date to his family or friends. In these ways it becomes increasingly difficult for a bachelor to remain open to possibilities. We take on the role cast for us and act "as if" because others expect it. It is sometimes easier to allow limits, even if doing so restricts options.

A woman involved with a bachelor therefore might engage in serious self-examination about how important marriage is to her. She can consider the sources of her social support, the degree to which she wants to combine her life with that of someone else, and the degree to which she values her independence. In particular, she might consider if she will be disappointed if the relationship does not lead to marriage. If she will be greatly disheartened to not be married, then she might be better off dating a man who has been divorced—a divorced man has gone to the altar (at least) once and therefore is more likely to marry again.

Marriage statistics do not tell us the complete story—the *quality* of a person's life is not considered. More important, many men have engaged in positive relationships that did not include marriage. At times our society has promoted marriage as having magical powers, which transform the participants so that they pass through mysterious gates with nirvana waiting on the other side. The reality is that marriage is a beginning, not an end. A marriage ceremony is a public acknowledgment of a couple's love for one another. Along with the affection that they express, the couple makes a commitment to uphold a contract of mutually beneficial emotional, physical, and financial support. Marriage holds forth great promise and potential, but it is not a panacea. If a person was miserable before marriage, he or she will probably be miserable after; if a person was content before marriage, he or she will probably continue to be so afterward.

People marry for all kinds of reasons, and some reasons are not so healthy. Unfortunately our society can put special pressure on women to become "whole," "complete," or "normal" by getting married and raising a family. From very early ages many girls are taught that success involves snagging "Mr. Right" and supporting his endeavors. Beginning with the childhood baby doll through the passive role of waiting for a proposal, society may inculcate into women the idea that their worth depends on adopting the roles of wife and mother. Special slurs—old maid and spinster—are reserved for women who remain single. These stigmas are bolstered by economic conditions that still do not reward women equally with men for doing the same job. This pressure makes marriage, for many women, more of a monetary necessity than a pleasurable opportunity.

If a woman's self-examination results in her realization that her desire to marry is propelled by early messages about a girl's role being to grow up and get married, or that financial pressures underlie her desire to join with a partner, she may want to fully explore her own potential to be self-supportive. Psychological studies consistently report that single women are happier than their married peers. Clearly, just like for her male counterpart, remaining single has the potential to be a viable lifestyle, which carries with it as much potential for fulfillment as any other lifestyle. For although marriage holds forth great hope, these benefits result from a *successful* marriage, *not* marriage per se.

Clues to the quality of a potential relationship with a bachelor may be gained by looking at and understanding the overall quality of this man's life and relationships. Bachelors are diverse. They vary regarding how they interact with people who are significant to them. Some men draw women into their lives and work at a relationship, while others vigorously maintain their solitude, viewing attempts at closeness as intrusions to be fought off. Important clues to a man's personal nature are revealed by first considering which bachelor personality type he is. Knowing whether he is Flexible, Conflicted, or Entrenched will help you understand what he is likely do in his relationship with you.

A Flexible bachelor holds the most obvious potential as a partner. He is more adept at relating comfortably and productively with others. Although self-reliant, he is most prepared to ease into a relationship based on mutuality of interests. Although the Flexible bachelor is committed to his independence and autonomy, he can relate to others in positive terms and tends to have deeper, longer, and more satisfying relationships with women. He is less likely than the other bachelors to become frightened by closeness and withdraw in hasty retreat. In addition, he is more likely to be self-confident and to have achieved more in his career. Although the Flexible bachelor has many needs for separateness, he is more likely to also relate to others well enough to feel satisfied, content, and whole. Somewhat paradoxically the self-fulfillment that makes Flexible bachelors potentially good partners also makes them less likely to marry: They have little urge to change. The irrelevance of marriage for these men, and their indifference to social customs in general, probably leads to continuing past patterns rather than developing new ones. Content as they are, Flexible bachelors tend to embrace their status quo.

Two eventualities may encourage the Flexible bachelor to marry. One circumstance would be when his pattern of indifference is disrupted. The death of a parent, sibling, or other relative or the loss of a job may lead a man to seriously re-evaluate his current situation. These disruptions need not be negative. For example, the birth of a niece or nephew or a job change that leads to his realization that he has finally "arrived" in his career may set major personal changes in motion. He may desire closeness, permanence, or a partner to join in his new endeavors. Since he is not intensely against marriage, he may wed.

The second circumstance that may encourage the Flexible bachelor to marry comes from internal drives. A Flexible man may get married when he is convinced that the advantages of such an arrangement outweigh the disadvantages. Unlike the Entrenched bachelor, the Flexible bachelor does not depend solely on isolation for his psychological well-being, but instead is relatively indifferent to being married. His nonchalance can be altered. The Flexible bachelor is most likely to get married after having spent a considerable amount of time testing (and retesting) the benefits and drawbacks that come with being with a particular woman. A long relationship including dating, spending time with her, and sharing a home will probably be needed before he makes a permanent commitment.

The bachelor type most likely to marry is the Conflicted bachelor. Dissatisfied, uncomfortable, and seeking change in his life, he feels the most desire to become closely involved with another person. He also has the most mixed experiences in relating to others. His desires for closeness and relatedness are real, but so are his fears of intrusions, demands, and loss of control. Conflicted men want relationships, but approach them with competing desires and fears. Finding a comfortable balance between these opposing feelings is demanding for people who are adept at getting along with others, but for the Conflicted man who is not so skilled at

relating to others, the task can be truly daunting. These relationships can be marked by separations, arguments, flight, and reconstruction as this man oscillates between clinging to his love and
pushing her out of his life.

The dilemma Conflicted men attempt to resolve in their relationships is similar to what psychologists refer to as the "schizoid
compromise." In this scenario the individual "hovers between two
opposite fears, the fear of isolation in independence with loss of
his ego in a vacuum of experience, and the fear of bondage to, of
imprisonment or absorption in the personality of whomsoever he
rushes to for protection" (Guntrip, 1969, p. 291). As noted earlier,
Conflicted bachelors readily recall relationships in which they felt
simultaneously attracted and repulsed. They vacillate between
moving toward and moving away from their lover. Reflecting on
their relationships, they are glad that they "kept their options open."

Making a commitment to marriage eliminates other possible
women or bachelorhood, and Conflicted men obsessively hold onto
their options. By not committing themselves fully to a relationship,
but not wanting to withdraw too far into isolation, Conflicted men
are quite equivocal. They can appear wishy-washy. They can also
drive women crazy with their mixed, often contradictory messages.
One day the Conflicted bachelor wants his girlfriend to move in,
and the next day he is not returning her phone calls. Duane spoke
of buying a baby carrier to carry his girlfriend's son on his bicycle
and then breaking up with her and returning the seat, unused,
within two weeks of its purchase. This mistreatment is not out of
any desire to hurt women, but this can be the result nevertheless.

Conflicted men's fears of being abandoned and alone or of
making a major, uncorrectable mistake are serious and cannot be
dismissed. Many bachelors have found an acceptable balance of
their competing needs, even though this may have been at the
expense of not taking risks, which may be more satisfying and less
compromising. Conflicted bachelors appear to establish a sense of
their own autonomy during their mid-twenties, settle into career
positions, and then stay there. Member of this group show some
flexibility in their adjustments and transitions during adulthood,
but are most likely to continue along whatever paths they began
before age 30; they do not want to disturb the equilibrium.

Conflicted bachelors may be the most likely to marry, but having
a successful marriage will be challenging. As is seen in the four-year

follow-up with Dean, Conflicted bachelors can become conflicted husbands. Their desire for closeness mixed with their fears of intrusion will not necessarily be shed when they get married. However, people can change and revise their approaches to relationships. The loving connection with a wife who supplies supportive challenges and yet is flexibly resolute can quiet the Conflicted bachelor's ambivalence so that he can be a fully intimate mate. Although these tasks may seem daunting, they are not unique to relationships with bachelors. In many ways the keys for a successful marriage to a Conflicted bachelor are the same as they are for any marriage. A Conflicted bachelor may be more entrenched in his ambivalence, more distant from his feelings, and more reserved in addressing his struggle, but he contends with experiences characteristic of many men.

Entrenched bachelors are a different story. These men are the least likely to get married. They are the most committed to staying single because their separateness actually keeps them satisfied. They show little or no desire for social involvement; they are content that their few needs are met. Entrenched men cut themselves off from rich experiences by shying away from others, avoiding relationships that would be too stimulating sexually or emotionally, behaving passively, and never aspiring too high in work or play. Through these maneuvers they maintain a level of personal comfort. Compared to most people, Entrenched bachelors have deficiencies in their capacity to form positive social connections, but they are content. As they withdraw from deep relationships and are inhibited in their ability to express their feelings, Entrenched bachelors are probably far less attractive to women than Flexible or Conflicted bachelors. At the same time an Entrenched bachelor may be less frustrating to an interested woman because he is consistent in stating his lack of intention to get seriously involved.

The Entrenched bachelor's diminished social competence makes him more readily identifiable as impoverished than the Flexible bachelor. It is not surprising that Entrenched bachelors have few close friends, like living alone, and have no desire to become parents themselves. When they describe relationships, it is more in terms of activities than of feelings. For instance, Ernie says, "We did a lot of things together, like planting the garden together," or Ernest relates, "It was good to have someone to go along on my trips with me." Entrenched bachelors are sometimes identifiable by the way they describe their early adulthood as having had little focus or direction. They invested little energy toward constructive vocational pursuits. They were "fuzzy" about what they wanted to do, with several reporting feeling "lost" throughout their twenties.

While recognizing that the experience of dating a never-married man will be different depending on his individual personality, some general recommendations for a woman who is currently involved with a bachelor, or who is considering becoming involved with one, are offered here. The most general observation has to do with a necessary underpinning of all successful relationships: the need for understanding, respect, and appreciation. It is a mistake to get into relationships with hidden plans to change the other person.

Although the realistic appraisal of a partner, recognizing both strengths and shortcomings, is necessary to build a positive relationship, sometimes we focus on one aspect of his or her personality that we wish was different. Once we find this fault, we can get so focused on the negative aspects of this attribute, and the need to alter it, that we lose the complete picture: Attention becomes so concentrated that this annoying trait becomes the whole person. For example, a couple is invited to a party. She has a higher level of sociability than he does, so after two hours he is ready to leave, but she is settling in and enjoying herself. Each person in this couple could focus on the other's "fault" in desiring to stay too long, or not long enough, and get upset. Or they can decide on a mutually agreeable solution such as driving two cars to accommodate different departure times.

With never-married men their relational "deficiency" is easy to identify: Their strong commitment to individualism, self-reliance, and autonomy makes deep intimacy difficult. However, these attributes are worthy of respect as well as concern. Rather than rushing to judge and find fault, and allowing these qualities to wreck the relationship, understanding these characteristics and placing them in context might allow one to see these men as diamonds in the rough. Many women find characteristics of independence and self-reliance desirable. A bachelor may be less controlling and have fewer expectations in relationships, leaving a woman free to actualize more of her own desires. If a woman can value the personality characteristics of such a man, rather than trying to change them, she may enjoy a genuinely sustaining relationship. For instance, bachelors are able to do things on their own; they are not highly dependent. They are not aggressive, demanding, or possessive men, but instead appear tolerant in letting other people make their own decisions. Bachelors do not act without forethought and deliberation. In addition, never-married men are more unconventional and may support divergent ways of behaving. Seen in these ways, some never-married men can combine in harmonious concert with the right women.

ENHANCING RELATIONSHIPS

Recommendations specific to growing in a relationship with a never-married man revolve around the following eight points:

- Work to understand him.
- Check out reality and chase down distortions.
- Value independence and express it.
- Go slow.
- Practice some distance.
- Do something together.
- Consider a non-traditional career.
- Do not rebuke yourself if the bachelor retreats.

First, as stressed above, *work to understand him*. Through understanding, getting to see the premium he places on self-reliance and autonomy, valuing can take place. You do not have to accept everything he does, but reacting to him without trying to know his perspective will end any hopes for a relationship. Work to see his actions from his perspective as well as your own. Sensitive understanding can be difficult to accomplish because it takes time, energy, and forbearance. However, since you are expecting (quite reasonably) these efforts from him, too, you might as well initiate and model what you hope to receive. Understanding also requires the ability to step back and get perspective on the situation, which can be difficult when you are caught up reacting to a particular behavior. Reading about the bachelor personality and the ways these men behave will help you gain perspective on him.

Understanding a never-married man further involves knowing his motivations. Appreciate that most behaviors are simultaneously determined by a variety of different impulses; they are not always related to something you did. If he pulls back from you, appreciate that this may be his standard way of getting along. Do not take these behaviors too personally. Keep a perspective on his statements so that you avoid feeling responsible for his projections and distortions. It may be easy to take personal affront to the way a bachelor interacts with you when he is responding more to something in him than in you. For instance, recognize that the bachelor's strong commitment to individualism and self-reliance was in place long before your relationship started. Therefore, his standoffishness and reluctance to place his welfare in your hands are not necessarily a statement about his feelings for you. If you interpret independent characteristics as a direct reflection of a lack of investment in the relationship, you may be misreading him and setting yourself up unnecessarily for heartbreak.

While it will usually be possible for you to understand his perspective, do not be afraid to ask another person to help you try to know what is going on in his head and heart. Talk with a female (or, better yet, male) friend, and have her or him help you put the bachelor's actions in perspective.

The second observation follows closely on the heels of the first: *Check out reality and chase down distortions.* Since never-married men often approach circumstances idiosyncratically, a successful relationship will include lots of reality checking, which allows apparent inconsistencies to be reconciled and misunderstandings to be clarified. For instance, a bachelor might feel that he is giving his girlfriend a lot of personal space for her own development, but she might experience this as indifference on his part. In order to avoid the hurt feelings on both sides that arise from misunderstandings, this couple needs to talk. Knowing how important personal freedom is to him is an important step in appreciating that he may think he is acting with your best interest at heart, but discussing and clarifying what each of you means by your actions and what you need and desire from one another are also important.

Time and again when interviewing bachelors about their relationships, many of their sentences begin with the phrase, "She made me do. . . . " This opening usually refers to feeling forced into some activity. The phrase sometimes appears with an ending that appears to be at odds with the sentence's beginning. For instance, "She made me take more time off from work," or "She made me eat more healthy food," or "She made me be more social than I would have been on my own." Bachelors seem to resist being directed even when it might be in their best interest.

There is no way of truly knowing the degree to which a girlfriend "forced" him to do something. However, given the passivity of many bachelors, a pattern of her initiating behavior and his following along submissively appears to be common. Bachelors seem to deny their own free will. The control bachelors presumed their girlfriends were exercising over them was probably less than these men would make it out to be. The "she made me" prelude may be a projection through which he ascribes responsibility to her, thereby denying his own volition. This kind of distortion needs to be understood and clarified. Couples who get cast rigidly in the roles of initiator and follower do not grow productively. One person always appears to be way ahead, and the other one is seen as behind.

Beyond the possible inequity in a relationship where she is always the initiator and he is invariably the follower, another danger in the "she made me" pattern is that this can be seen as a reason why he has to flee the relationship. He will pull back either overtly by breaking up or covertly by limiting his involvement. The "she made me" pattern needs to be understood in terms of the distortion and misrepresentation that it might be. Bachelors need to take responsibility for their own needs, wishes, and behaviors. Changing a bachelor's perception of himself as follower to co-initiator—increasing his sense of choice in the couple's activities— will go a long way to keep a couple growing to mature levels. By so doing, a bachelor will be less inclined to feel that his personal control and prerogatives have been usurped. Therefore, work periodically as a couple to understand what is a suggestion, a request, or a demand. This process can help each partner feel less threatened and more in control.

The best way to check out reality and chase down distortions is to confront them directly with the man involved. However, this can be difficult with the never-married man, who would rather avoid discussing feelings. You may need to initiate and insist on this interaction, but keep in mind that he may lack the words to express his emotional reaction. Couples often find it helpful to set aside a regular, specific time to discuss what is going on between them. Without a set time these important discussions get neglected.

Conversations should affirm positive aspects of the relationship as well as dealing with negative facets.

The third recommendation about becoming involved with a bachelor is to *value independence and express it.* If you have to pretend that you value independence, then you are with the wrong man, and you ought to move on. However, if you, like your bachelor friend, value independence, you should express this position to him in no uncertain terms. Independence is one of the attributes that he values highly, so it is important that he hears you endorse it as well. This may seem rather obvious, and you might feel that you are already doing this, but many people overestimate their overt support of their partners' beliefs.

Sometimes we are reluctant to endorse what is important to others for fear that they will take this as license to run amuck. A woman may feel that because her boyfriend is so committed to independence and self-reliance, she must uphold the opposite position to pull him back to center. The visual image for this activity is a tug-of-war. The result is constant tension, a perpetual battle. The paradox of this endeavor (as in so many human relations) is that a person often gets what she wants from a partner when she gives up the struggle to pull him over to her side. When you also value independence, you will let him know that he is not left as the only standard bearer for independence. He will be less likely to vigorously defend his position. He will be more willing to compromise his independence and join you. Letting go of your end of the rope can be scary, but after initial, off-balance fumbling around, people can both move to the center and yield their extreme positions.

Relationships with bachelors will probably be best when they proceed slowly. The fourth observation, therefore, is to *go slow.* Going slow has most to do with that funny phase in a relationship after the initial flurry of romantic excitement when everything seems ideal and full of possibilities. Rather than everything being easy, the need for negotiations, for give-and-take, arises. This can take place after four days, four weeks, or four months depending on the couple. During this phase a couple shifts from the initial exhilarated excitement to a period of more realistic appraisal of the relationship's potential. More complicated considerations of needs and wants begin at this time. Obstacles can be encountered when exorbitant hopes overtake reason; disappointments inevitably result. Remaining realistic and proceeding deliberately, but patiently, offer hope for growing intimacy with a never-married man. Quick, furtive attempts to reconcile differences will probably be met with opposition. Bachelors need time to understand and work out their experiences. At the same time trying to sweep disagreements under the carpet sets a bad precedent.

Properly pacing a new relationship takes discipline. Often we feel exhilarated and want to race headlong into closer connections. Conversely, going too slowly can doom a relationship. When relationships involve bachelors, a misunderstanding is most likely to result when the woman is interested in pursuing a deeper relationship at a pace faster than he is comfortable with. Problems can ensue when one member's hopes about cultivating more from the relationship are different from the other's. She may feel confused and discouraged by his sedate approach to the situation. Confusion and discouragement are two separate problems and need to be addressed differently.

Confusion can be addressed by inviting the man to explain the motives underlying his actions. She can then clarify communications by letting him know what message she received. For instance, he might fail to call her at work when she was hoping that he would, leaving her feeling that he does not care. However, asking him about it might reveal his intent to respect her privacy. With this understanding on the table she can state how she feels about his calling and then let him include this new awareness in his future actions.

Some women may get discouraged by the relationship's pace. This is a more complicated issue. If proceeding slowly is intolerable, then she might admit that this is not the man for her. But there may be benefits to pacing relationships differently than she has in the past. Factors extraneous to the relationship are often responsible for rushing a sense of connectedness along at a devil-may-care speed. For instance, a woman may feel pressured by the ticking of her biological clock, feel isolated because a close friend was transferred, or fear that this is her last chance to get married. These factors, whether real or irrational, lead to placing pressures on the relationship that it cannot sustain. But remember that distortion thrives in haste. Taking the time to realistically review the advantages and disadvantages of this relationship with this man and then either deciding he is worth it or dumping him and moving on may save a great deal of heartache down the road.

The fifth recommendation, to *practice some distance* in the relationship, has to do with acting on the value you place on independence. Having recognized the advantages of self-reliance and acknowledged these feelings to your bachelor friend, now it is time to act on these beliefs. Keep your own apartment. Maintain your own friends and activities. Do not sit around waiting for his phone call to let you know his plans. This does not mean that you are indifferent to him and his needs, but you do want to show that your life is not contingent on him for your every decision. If you are too dependent on him, you will both end up either separate from one another or very miserable together.

Must a woman involved with a never-married man passively wait for him to initiate activity? Not necessarily. However, a woman might be most successful if she follows the sixth suggestion, that the couple *do something together*. The emphasis here is on *doing* something together: engaging in an activity together rather than focusing directly on the relationship. Most men are more doers than talkers, more instrumental than emotional. Suggesting that you *do* something together may make him feel more at ease and more eager to interact. Plant a garden together, go to a ball game, camp in a national forest, canoe down a river, or paint a room together; do whatever might allow you both to connect in a way that is comfortable to him. Relating through these activities on a concrete level rather than on a more emotional plane plays to his strengths.

Some women might scoff at this suggestion, feeling that they do not have to engage in activities in order to achieve intimacy. These women see open conversation and shared emotions as necessary and sufficient to promote strong bonds. While these are certainly necessary, whether they are sufficient is questionable. Also, there may be more than one way to get where you want to go. A woman who can meet a man "in his world," where relating is enhanced through physical proximity and shared interaction, also increases the likelihood of his joining "her world" of deep intimacy through personal self-disclosure. Therefore, to reach connectedness, try letting him be on familiar ground. If this makes you uncomfortable, then perhaps it can increase your empathy for him when he comes into the world of feelings, where you are the expert. Instead of battling over who is doing what to satisfy whom, let these activities be satisfying to both of you. The cooperation, mutuality, sharing, and respect that are enhanced through shared projects should carry over into other areas of the relationship as well.

Another aid to achieving happy involvement with a bachelor might be to *consider a non-traditional career*. Do not quit your job and find a new career, but consider that a bachelor might be more comfortable with a girlfriend or wife whose lifestyle helps maintain lives that are not constantly intertwined. Working as a flight attendant or a retail buyer, which requires you to spend a good deal of time traveling, may be an asset to your relationship, giving both you and him the freedom and flexibility you desire. A position as a news reporter, night manager, or professional musician might keep you out of the house when he is there and allow each of you to maintain a deeper relationship during the time periods you have together.

The last recommendation has more to do with you as an individual than it does with constructive approaches to the relationship itself: *Do not rebuke yourself if the bachelor retreats*. If the relationship ends, do not quickly excuse him and condemn yourself. Although it is important to review and learn from your role in a relationship so that you can take responsibility for what you contributed to it, consider the relationship within the context of *his* life, too. Do not take the whole blame yourself; even if you do everything right, some relationships still do not work. Nor should they. Some relationships are better when spoken of in the past tense. In addition, although women are more often entrusted with keeping relationships going, they must not lose sight that responsibility for a healthy relationship is shared by both partners.

Why do some people exaggerate their sense of personal responsibility for a breakup? Sometimes taking too much blame for the end of a relationship indicates a desire for control. This reasoning follows the pattern of "If I am responsible for what went on in this last situation, then I can make it go the way I want it to next time." This is irrational—each relationship is independent from all others. Although an initial false sense of control can be gratifying, it is illusory and will inevitably crash down on a person. Getting into relationships means relinquishing control and jurisdiction. This is part of the fun and growth in relationships when it means sharing new ideas, attitudes, and undertakings. When relationships become unsafe or painful, however, not being in control can be miserable—but there is little we can do about it.

The recommendations offered here are not commandments (because then there would be ten of them), but are constructive suggestions meant to augment the other skills that you and your friend bring to your relationship. These recommendations may be most helpful if you review and modify them together, taking those that appear useful to your particular situation and personalizing them to fit your relationship's needs.

NOTE

1. These figures may also be misleading regarding heterosexual single men, as the census data do not distinguish between these and gay single men.

11

NOTES FOR BENEFITTING FROM PSYCHOTHERAPY

Bachelors, like other single persons, seek psychological services to a greater extent than do their married peers. This high prevalence may be due to the bachelors internalizing society's questions about whether they are normal. It may also be that bachelors struggle more in their lives because of the additional burdens of taking on life's demands without a partner. At the same time bachelors probably also seek psychological services due to the limitations inherent in relying on immature defense mechanisms. Conflicted bachelors, in particular, seek therapy because their ambivalent feelings about serious relationships—being drawn toward marriage while simultaneously fleeing from it—wreak havoc on their psychological well-being.

The good news is that psychotherapy is available and has great potential benefit for bachelors. Lots of evidence suggests that psychotherapy can help resolve both specific and general bachelor concerns (e.g., Mental health, 1995; Smith, Glass, & Miller, 1980). Unfortunately, both sexes, but even more so men, tend to resist psychotherapy because it feels foreign and threatening. In fact, the very process that makes individual therapy successful contrasts with many bachelor personality traits. At the same time this discrepancy between psychotherapy and bachelor traits means that psychotherapy can be very enlightening for bachelors who can fully engage in it. Bachelors can benefit from what is both *said* and *done* in therapy: Everything about how the therapeutic interaction is construed can help bachelors meet life's challenges. However, because the tasks can be unfamiliar, bachelors can flee treatment prematurely.

This chapter is intended as a brief primer to help bachelors consider ways to make optimal use of individual psychotherapy. Psychotherapy is most successful when it is approached with the right frame of reference. The observations put forth here begin with general comments about what makes psychotherapy especially helpful in dealing with life's problems. Observations are then offered to help bachelors see how they can use psychotherapy in ways that expand on their core bachelor tendencies.[1]

Too often psychotherapy is ill-fated because people consider it akin to a visit to a medical doctor. However, there are important differences. In a medical intervention the patient is relatively passive: It is the doctor's task to diagnose the patient and make him[2] well. The cause of medical problems is often quickly surmised, generally identified with demonstrable physical evidence, which leads to swift, decisive intervention. Medical treatment, if it is going to be effective, often works quickly, and though it is sometimes prolonged, the patient's personal emotions have little to do with its results.

By contrast in psychological intervention the client is very active: The therapist's task is to help the client become more expressive about his problem(s) so that the client will better understand himself and his actions. The client brings within him to the therapeutic encounter many of the resources and strengths that will be called on to collaboratively improve the client's life. Although hypothetical causes of psychological problems can often be formulated, direct physical evidence supporting their authenticity is usually not available: Causality is often complex and unconscious. Swift, decisive intervention can be successful, but more sustaining results are usually gained within the context of an evolving therapeutic relationship. During the intervention progress can sometimes seem illusory, and therapy can be stormy. Psychological treatment, though sometimes featuring quick initial benefits, can be prolonged for full effectiveness. In psychotherapy the patient's personal feelings have everything to do with the results.

Psychotherapy can be uniquely helpful because it is a social relationship without the usual social rules. For instance, in psychological treatment any feelings and thoughts that come to the patient's mind should be voiced. Unlike many social interactions, which have built-in rules for what is "proper," unrestricted speech is encouraged in therapy because whatever is on the client's mind may contribute to finding better solutions to his problems. The therapeutic relationship supports this free expression of ideas because it is artificially constructed and therefore can be free from normal social judgments.

Seeing things from the client's perspective and helping him better know how particular actions fit into his overall undertakings are possible because the therapist's only investment is in trying to help the client better understand himself and act in his own best interest. People who interact in the client's "real" world may be invested in the client acting in certain ways—whether or not these actions are in the client's best interest. Because the therapeutic relationship is not complicated by additional relationships, which may compromise the interaction, therapists are able to unconditionally support a client who undertakes personal risks to live better. The uniqueness of the therapeutic relationship permits the suspension of usual social expectations so that explicit and implicit reinforcement for changes can be offered and assistance in better understanding specific actions, altering activities, and overcoming deficits can be addressed. The fact that confidentiality and privacy are rigorously maintained in psychotherapy also promotes being honest and open with whatever comes to mind.

Another social convention that is suspended in psychotherapy is that psychotherapists rarely give advice. Many people expect to tell a therapist about a problem and then have her or him give advice that will solve everything immediately. However, life just does not work like that. Advice is cheap; there is no reason to pay for it. Lots of people are ready to give advice; in fact, a person has probably sought and dismissed a lot of advice before he enters psychotherapy. If advice is all that is needed, people would not be paying for professional treatment. Rather than spending most of their time lecturing clients with sage advice, psychotherapists are more likely to be listening actively to what the client has to say. As they listen, therapists point out deficits or contradictions that they observe.

How does listening help? For one thing it allows the client to fully explore his problems. People who are quick to offer their own input rarely get the full sense of what is really at the heart of a problem. In this way good, non-judgmental listening makes problems more understandable so that solutions come to the forefront. By accurately organizing and clarifying the predicament through active listening, it becomes more manageable, and resolution becomes possible. Good listening also helps a person feel less alone with a concern: This support helps foster a sense of hope.

Clients often need to train themselves to say whatever comes to their minds. Clients will often censor their thoughts or try to guess what the therapist really wants to know. They must come to trust that the therapist will use what is said to help the client rather than somehow using his uncensored statements against him, as can be the case in other social encounters. Good therapists have no preconceived notions about what is right or what is wrong or what the best solution is until the client begins to observe the advantages for himself. One great advantage of talking with a psychotherapist is that she or he has no "ax to grind." The therapist has no personal investment in the decisions clients make for themselves. She or he just wants to understand, with you, why you do things and how you might better achieve your goals.

At times it may seem that your therapist expects you to act in a certain way. However, good therapists are attuned to be sure that their clients are getting what they really want for themselves. Most people have problems making decisions because they do not know enough. Therefore, therapists see their task as giving clients the opportunity to talk things over with someone who does not try to make decisions for them. During this process the therapist will sometimes make you aware of when you are kidding yourself. Most of us are not always fully honest with ourselves, but it can be embarrassing when someone points out how two things we are doing do not fit together. The job of your therapist is to help you keep in mind all of your important facts and feelings so that you can come to a solution that takes all of this information into account. It is hard because sometimes your feelings conflict; then again, if life was not complex, you would not be human.

Beyond a psychotherapist who listens and works to fully understand the client's experience, what else makes psychotherapy work? In general, we might break psychological treatment's effectiveness into six general "curative factors." This is not an all-inclusive list, but it gives some insight into how psychotherapy promotes positive mental health. The first way in which psychotherapy can be helpful is by promoting *constructive self-observation*. People who see themselves clearly can better recognize patterns in which they engage, understand their own roles within problems, and do something to change themselves and their circumstances. A second curative factor can be *catharsis*: the process of getting one's feelings out. There are many sanctions in our society against releasing feelings, but sometimes the healthy way is to give these feelings full expression. The word *catharsis* comes from the Greek meaning "to purify," which connects with the personal growth that happens when repressed emotions are discharged. *Knowledge* is a third curative factor. Knowledge takes many forms depending on the client's needs and the therapist's orientation. Gaining knowledge within psychotherapy can involve finding a language with which to better understand a problem, discerning causes, exploring options, revealing consequences, normalizing feelings or experiences, and enhancing social skills. Knowledge can also involve getting explicit strategies to redress specific problems.

Insight is a special kind of knowledge, which can be a fourth curative factor. Insight involves understanding patterns, which are being repeated, by connecting past experiences with present undertakings. Insight can also involve connecting internal needs with external experiences and understanding distortions, which may occur because personal needs are clouding one's view. A fifth curative factor is the *corrective emotional experience* that clients can experience in psychotherapy. By providing patients with acceptance, honesty, and an empathic understanding of their experiences, rather than judging and evaluating what they say, therapists provide growth-enhancing conditions, which may be missing in other areas of their clients' lives. These positive communication styles can serve as models for promoting productive relationships outside of therapy. A final curative factor is the *support* that therapists offer their clients. Because psychotherapists can provide deep understanding and emotional support, as well as aiding new efforts at meeting life's challenges, clients try harder, since they do not feel alone in their endeavors. As human beings we tend to make a greater effort when we undertake tasks as part of a team rather than on our own.

All these curative factors are best brought about within the context of a positive therapeutic relationship, which is marked by a therapists having sincere respect for the client, while working for an empathic understanding of the client's world. The more important of these qualities is the therapist's respect for her or his client. Therapists must accept their clients, or at least suspend whatever judgment they have of the client, so that unconditional positive regard is present. Explicit praise and punishment connected to particular actions is usually not part of the treatment process; instead, the client's basic humanity is recognized and valued. When these conditions are met, the therapeutic relationship will be felt by the client as a safe and dependable place, which models healthy relationships, allows for intense feelings to be experienced, and motivates the client to bring about positive personal change.

So does having this positive therapeutic relationship mean that a client will be friends with his therapist? Although you should feel an openness toward your therapist and be treated with dignity and respect, it is not appropriate to act as if you are best friends with your therapist. In fact, although you may feel like you would like to continue your therapy session at a local tavern over a beer, doing so would be problematic. For one thing having a beer at a tavern ought to be a mutually satisfying social encounter. In psychotherapy, by contrast, attention is necessarily unequally focused on the client. Also, psychotherapy should be comfortable and engaging, but also challenging and demanding. Although not every session has to be extremely intense, you should feel accountable for your feelings and actions when in treatment. Therapy's focused attention is designed to take place during specified times of limited duration.

Although elements of friendship are there, thinking that your therapist is your best friend may indicate that she or he is not confronting you enough or helping you redress your shortcomings. Psychologist D. W. Winnicott (1972) wrote that good therapy is a process of "holding and shaping." "Holding" is the sensitive, unconditionally accepting manner in which the therapist treats each client with dignity and respect. "Shaping," on the other hand, has to do with those actions your therapist undertakes to help you move away from your present problems to a more productive, satisfying life. Too much holding or too much shaping is not productive for the overall growth process. We need to be treated with dignity and respect, but as human beings we also grow by being challenged appropriately. As a client, you can monitor the degree to which you are feeling held or shaped by your therapist. If you do not feel an appropriate balance of these two elements, state this to your therapist, and see what can be done about it.

It may help to take on the attitude that you are paying your therapist to be like a business "consultant" hired to counsel your company. Like a business consultant, your therapist is invested in your improvement, but you have ultimate say over what is undertaken, and you are responsible for whatever changes take place. However, in business when a company hires someone to *consult*, that person is often seen as someone hired to *insult*. We expect them to find fault and recommend major transformations. Psychotherapy is different because of the ongoing nature of the relationship. Meeting on a regular basis allows for change to be adopted in the context of continued interacting and monitoring. When consultants come into companies, they are usually given a specific fee, so it is in their best interest to conduct a quick evaluation, issue a report, and exit as soon as possible.

Consultants also want to leave the impression that they have made a contribution, so they often leave behind sweeping recommendations for reform. Sometimes these encyclopedic plans overlook the strengths and assets of a functioning group. This is an error in judgment that well-trained psychotherapists avoid. Also, since outside paid consultants are hired by management, they often err on the side of management. Although they may objectively examine the entire organization, they will often make pointed recommendations that distort the focus in order to protect the managers. After all, business consultants want to be hired again or recommended to other organizations. A difference in psychotherapy is that the client is both the manager *and* the worker. You hire and decide when to release your outside consultant.

The following guidelines are offered to counter the core bachelor personality characteristics and tendencies in order to make the best use of personal psychotherapy. Psychotherapy is challenging. Psychotherapy can be difficult. But when approached energetically, it can be quite illuminating and rejuvenating. When you want to examine some of your basic assumptions about life and learn new ways to interact, psychotherapy is the best game in town. To really get the most from psychotherapy, bachelors would do well to

- Be active.
- Depend on their therapist.
- Be emotional.
- Be specific.
- Terminate intentionally.

BE ACTIVE

Most bachelors tend to be tentative and cautious. Although many confidently apply themselves in their careers, they tend to be hesitant when approaching others. There is certainly a place for passivity in some aspects of life, but shying away from too many situations does not promote growth. There is very little reason to be interpersonally passive in psychotherapy. In fact, psychotherapy is best approached with an active stance in which clients express personal feelings and recognize that talking about troublesome feelings can be useful. Psychotherapy becomes an opportunity to behave on the assertive end of life's spectrum. You will also have the opportunity to reflect on how constructive this position is for you. For example, bringing up concerns you have about the therapy process at a session assertively makes the best use of your treatment. Because of the artificial nature of the therapeutic relationship, you have nothing to lose by being direct with your therapist in ways that you feel may be harmful in other social encounters.

A first opportunity to approach psychotherapy actively comes in finding the right therapist. The best referrals come from friends and colleagues who report successful experiences with a particular clinician. However, you can also shop around. Visit one or two therapists. Talk with each of them. Find someone with whom you feel comfortable, but who will make you accountable for your actions in a way that will not make you too defensive. Find someone you can respect. Choose a therapist who has an active membership in a national professional organization so that you know she or he is accountable to a professional code of ethics.[3] Ask about her or his approach to treatment. Find a therapist who takes a psychodynamic, or psychoanalytically informed, approach to problems. These clinicians will be best prepared to explore all of the curative factors with you. However, just because they have this general approach, cognitive and behavioral strategies can also be part of your treatment. Activities to promote personal assertiveness are often indicated for bachelors. Sometimes assertiveness training is the major focus of therapy; at other times it is an initial element of the treatment, which facilitates growth in other areas.

While looking for a therapist, consider that you are looking not for the *perfect* therapist, but instead for one who is *good enough*. By good enough I mean someone with whom you have an adequate fit so that together you can move toward achieving your goals. Just like a good marriage, positive therapeutic relations are "made," not "found." Much of the pain and misfortune that bemuse us comes from searching for "perfection" instead of recognizing that "close" counts in more than horseshoes and hand grenades; good effort also counts in parenting, friendships, and psychotherapy. In these latter areas good results are created by sustained, collaborative efforts, not simply good initial fit.

Once you are in therapy, take full advantage of the therapeutic relationship to thoroughly explore the complete parameters of your life. Try new things. Be active in taking risks. Do not settle for the status quo. Consider alternatives. Try new activities. These endeavors should be easier because there is someone else in your corner pulling with you this time.

Be inquisitive in your therapy. Express yourself. Run on at the mouth. As you are curious about anything happening in your life, bring your questions into therapy. Remember your dreams and share them with your therapist. Ask direct questions of your therapist as they come to mind. As you wonder about your therapist's plans, inquire. Bachelors may avoid such temptations, perhaps thinking that they must respect their therapists' privacy. However, therapists can set their own boundaries—you are not responsible for them. Clients often imagine that a therapist will divulge pertinent information in her or his own good time. But the truth is that if the client is wondering about something, the time is ripe to address it.

At times therapists delay answering direct questions because they feel that exploring the client's underlying motivations and fantasies about the answer is more important than gratifying an impulse by answering the question. Many therapists may not ever fully answer all your questions. But good therapists eventually answer direct questions that are pertinent to your growth as a client. You may never know how many children your therapist has, what her favorite hobbies are, what kind of family he grew up in, or even what her marital status is. But, quite frankly, these are side issues to your development. What is more central is knowing what your curiosities say about you. After all, are you paying all this money to get to know your therapist or yourself? In fact, if your therapist talks too much about herself or himself, it is time to find a new therapist. I have had clients who at the end of successful treatment say, "You know, I don't know many facts about your life, but I feel like I really know you because of how well you have treated me."

DEPEND ON YOUR THERAPIST

One of the defining personality traits of bachelors is their allegiance to independence and self-reliance. Bachelors pride themselves on being self-reliant. They highly value their autonomy. The specter of giving up their freedom is unattractive to them. This vigilant defense of their independence shuts many bachelors off to the possibility of joining in valuable consort with others.

The caution bachelors exercise with regard to entrusting others with their welfare runs counter to some of the real advantages of psychotherapy. Therapists can be potentially beneficial consultants, but their input is only as valuable as clients allow it to be. Bachelors may compromise the potential effectiveness of treatment by limiting the degree to which they allow themselves to be affected by therapists. Clients benefit best when they are open to self-examination. The best client thinks about his therapist's input without swallowing everything hook, line, and sinker. He looks forward to discussing material with his therapist without being too controlling about how the session is spent. And the client who gets the most for his money allows his therapist to be important in his life. Part of the allure and success of personal psychotherapy is that the client can both depend on his therapist *and* maintain personal independence. The distinct boundaries that your therapist sets up around the relationship and her or his commitment to respect your personal integrity ensure that you can rely on your therapist without having to compromise your position to keep her or him happy.[4]

Psychotherapy therefore becomes a safe opportunity to practice depending on another person. If desired, what is learned from this experience can be transferred to other relationships. The positive experience practiced and examined in psychotherapy will make your next experience with allowing yourself to appropriately depend on someone else that much easier. In these ways psychotherapy becomes a significant forum within which to accept people as important allies, friends, and consorts.

It is no accident that your therapist is dependable: Recognizing that trust is a factor critical to facilitating a client's growth, a big part of the psychotherapist's training is to be reliable. She or he has also been prepared to watch for your signs of unhealthy dependence and to work to eliminate them. Your psychotherapist will maintain a healthy level of inter-reliance through self-monitoring and listening to the clues you send.

But how will you, as a patient, know that your psychotherapist is dependable? That knowledge will not come from your therapist admonishing you about how much she can be counted on. Nor will it be guesswork. Instead, your therapist will show that she is dependable by acting reliably: She will be consistently respectful, steadily promoting your growth and dignity in all she does. A reliable therapist will deliver on what she promises. If she says she will bring you some material to read, she will have it available; if she expresses interest in how you are handling a particular situation, she will follow up on it. She will remember certain details of your life, like the names of friends and family.

A therapist on whom you can rely will listen intently and ask questions when something is unclear. A dependable therapist will also be emotionally available and emotionally attentive: She will be sensitive to what is important to you. She will also confront you about discrepancies between what you say and what you do; she will notice when you are working at cross-purposes to yourself. By not letting you off the hook, a therapist demonstrates how she expects you to be your best and believe that you can achieve your goals. A reliable therapist wants you to live up to your full potential. Finally, unlike many other health-care providers, a reliable therapist will be on time for appointments, or she will contact you to make alternative plans. If you find your therapist lacking these qualities, address her directly about your concerns. If you confront your therapist, think of it as another learning experience: Be cognizant of your reactions because making another person aware of your experience, and working to resolve any discrepancies, is what psychotherapy (and all relationships for that matter) is all about.

Another way to consider the matter of depending on your therapist comes down to this question: Why not depend on him or her? What do you really have to lose? Psychotherapists can touch your emotional life, but their real influence in other important areas remains quite limited. Therefore, the therapeutic enterprise becomes an avenue to suspend typical ways of getting along in the world and instead to rely on someone else in healthy, adaptive ways. In the same manner that we heap special praise upon the ailing major league pitcher who puts his trust in rehabilitation specialists to return to his old (or better) form, there is something commendable about a person who appropriately depends on a psychotherapist for psychological reconditioning.

BE EMOTIONAL

Bachelors are emotionally guarded people. They are unlikely to display rich and vivid emotional lives. At times they may seem like they have no feelings or are detached from their feelings.

One of the greatest potential benefits of psychotherapy is that bachelors can experience the full range of their emotional lives. Good psychotherapists promote this encounter because they know that many of life's problems are caused by repressing feelings. By holding emotions inside, they do not get sorted out and understood; they get bottled up, cluttered, and confused. The more unclear these sensations are, the harder they are to articulate. It is only when emotions are given full expression that they can be appreciated. Once feelings are intelligible, they can be acted on directly and purposefully.

Even in psychotherapy bachelors may be tempted to restrain and retard their emotions. But a question similar to others asked in this chapter emerges: What is gained by repeating emotional repression in psychotherapy? The answer once again is that there is a lot to be gained (and little to lose) by attempting to be different in therapy. Therefore, share your feelings with your therapist. Put yourself in situations that make you emotional—watch romantic movies, interact with children, be with your family, leaf through old photo albums—and recount your feelings with your therapist. Push yourself to share on a deep level. Talk about old hurts and lost dreams. When talking about bygone feelings, try to get in touch with how these relate to your life at this moment. Proclaim new loves. Share emerging hopes. Speak of extended wishes. Be brutally honest about your feelings, whether they are positive or negative, whether you are proud or ashamed of them. Do not try to protect your therapist by sanitizing your emotions; after all, you pay your therapist to take what you have to dish out. If you feel like you are getting nowhere, express these concerns, too. Like all your feelings, these irritations can be dealt with in consultation with your therapist.

As mentioned in Chapter 9, sometimes emotions can be frightening to men because they get in touch with their anger. Men get concerned that their hostility will be dangerous. However, most people find that if they are able to give verbal expression to their feelings, they are less likely to act on them. Therefore, if you feel angry, express your rancor verbally. Then track down the source of this fervor so your understanding can lead you to handle it in mature ways. Psychotherapists have lots of practice fielding hostility and working to understand it. Therefore, you can feel safe in exposing your indignation. Realizing that there are adaptive and maladaptive ways of expressing anger, hostility, resentment, and aggression is part of learning to be a fully functioning adult.

Giving full expression to feelings is enhanced by knowing that personal psychotherapy is a time to be unabashedly self-focused. Therapy is your time to talk about whatever is of interest to you. Indulge yourself. Therapy is best when you are able to reflect on your life, and the first step is for you to make statements about your life so that you and your therapist will have data to analyze. Too often bachelors can be passive onlookers to their own lives. Within psychotherapy you can practice being an active contributor to your own destiny. You can learn, for instance, that some difficulties are self-inflicted, that you often waste a lot of time waiting for other people to act first, that some physical ailments are caused by psychological stresses, and, most important, that your greatest potential comes when you know yourself fully. As you talk about your feelings, you will probably learn that difficulties in living are common and that they can be dealt with effectively by talking about them with others.

So it behooves bachelors to get excited about self-exploration. In doing so, some men may fear that psychotherapy is making them overly narcissistic or too self-centered for anyone's good. However, unless this was the problem that brought you in for psychotherapy in the first place, it is unlikely that psychotherapy will create this problem within you. What usually happens is that therapy helps you find more of a balance between your outer (or objective) and inner (or subjective) experiences. Constructive personal life change is more likely to occur as you learn to recognize discordant situations and your subjective reactions to them. When you deal in an exploratory manner with your own subjective experiences and differentiate your reactions from the more objective reality of a situation, you are better equipped to deal effectively with life's challenges.

BE SPECIFIC

Idiosyncratic thinking, seeing things in novel ways, is another prominent bachelor style. Distortions among never-married men mostly arise from vague or inarticulate communication. Psychotherapy offers the opportunity for bachelors to clarify their communication, to specify and articulate differences, and to delineate and appreciate details. Bachelors can learn to recognize their own amorphous communication style. When this does not come easily, the psychotherapist can aid the process.

One of the ways in which psychotherapy can be helpful is that the therapist can act as a mirror (or complement) to help the client consider life concerns from a different modality. For instance, if a person's usual style is to approach life rationally, his therapist may get him to look at the more irrational or emotional aspects of a situation; if a client is usually global in his approach, the therapist may invite him to examine specific aspects of a situation. By using a variety of vantage points, the potential for constructive problem resolution is maximized. In successful therapy the client internalizes these new ways of considering challenges so that he has more ways to approach his personal problems.

One of my clients, an avid golfer, described his experience in psychotherapy as learning to "play with all 14 clubs in the golf bag."

For most of his life he used only two clubs—a driver and a putter—as he would erupt with feeling and then try to tenderly smooth things over. Because of our work together he learned to appreciate the subtle advantages of other approaches to life. He became more adept at using some of the "mid-range" clubs and, modulating his personal interactions, got along far better with others. (His golf game got better, too.)

Being specific helps bachelors better understand their own positions. As they practice clarifying themselves and being articulate about their observations, they will become more adept at achieving personal goals. Psychotherapists will help bachelors overcome their natural tendency toward disclarity and vagueness. For instance, instead of allowing a client to state, "I didn't really like her" when talking about a recent date, the therapist can help a client focus on specific aspects of the disinterest. Instead of allowing him to stop at "I think I might be good at that job," the therapist will ask the client to stipulate particular personal attributes that would be promoted by the new undertaking. At first the client may feel these attempts at clarification are intrusive and demanding. This is a common reaction to anything new and unfamiliar. However, recognizing the purpose of these questions, and considering that sometimes the caddie's suggestion to use a 5-iron rather than a driver ought to be heeded, makes therapist's observations easier to consider.

TERMINATE INTENTIONALLY

When is the right time to terminate psychotherapy? That needs to be negotiated on an individual basis, but for the most part you end therapy when your goals have been reached or you have new tools to work toward your goals on your own. Sometimes you end therapy when you feel you have not made any progress toward your goals in the last three months; but before progress is that stunted, you and your therapist should be working to get the train back on track.

Bachelors may tend to terminate abruptly and prematurely. Therefore, when you initially feel like quitting a therapy relationship that you think has been positive, do not do so in haste. Give yourself at least a few more sessions to discuss directly what is going on for you in therapy. At times you might feel that you are not getting anywhere—maybe that your therapist is a fool—and there is no point to therapy. These feelings often indicate that you may be preparing to work on something that is going to be challenging to you. You may have met what we refer to as "resistance." During these times it is good to remember your overall commitment to personal change through psychotherapy so that these temporary feelings do not overtake your better thoughts about personal change and stop you from going through with modifications that, although difficult, are in your best interest.

Some people terminate psychotherapy abruptly as soon as their goals are reached because they cannot handle the mixed feelings about stopping therapy. Ending therapy brings out the positive feelings of your "graduating" and moving on to better things, but on the negative side you are also saying goodbye to someone who is valuable to you. Ironically, it is often when your therapeutic relationship is most positive, and things are going just right for you, that it is time to end treatment. It helps to anticipate that terminating may not be easy. As with any feelings you have, it helps to talk about your concerns about ending as soon as these feelings come up. Preparing for the ending makes the joining more possible; people often hold back early in relationships as a way to protect themselves from what might come later—but these people end up leading limited, stunted lives.

There are many advantages to terminating psychotherapy intentionally and deliberately. This is not the only time in your life when relationships come to an end, but this might be the best time to do it "right." Doing it "right" means experiencing loss and change without having to retreat from these feelings. Recognizing that growth involves losing old ways of being, you will deal with these losses in constructive ways and demonstrate for yourself that all feelings, even sad and hurtful ones, can be talked about. These opportunities can best be actualized if you hang in there and do not "vote with your feet" by unilaterally quitting treatment.

Circumventing premature termination may also be aided by anticipating what your areas of resistance may be so that you can work through them and achieve your goals. Flexible bachelors are least likely to seek personal psychotherapy, but if they do, they may become competitive with their therapists rather than depending on them. Flexible bachelors often join others through shared activities rather than deep emotional involvement. Therefore, they may resist struggling with feelings about love and marriage. They may feel psychotherapy is too controlling or smothering. The therapeutic task for Flexible bachelors may be to establish that their interpersonal needs can be met without becoming personally suffocated.

Entrenched bachelors are also unlikely to seek psychotherapy, but at times their confused, disconnected feelings may bring them in. Their goal will be to see that their personal integrity is not as markedly threatened by interpersonal contact as they imagine. Getting in touch with needy feelings can be arduous for Entrenched bachelors. Entrenched bachelors may flee treatment by complaining that it is too intrusive and demanding, or that they just do not see what the point of it is. Knowing that they are securely independent, even when they express their personal desire for connectedness and interrelatedness, will be important for them if they are to tolerate psychotherapy.

Conflicted bachelors struggle with personal crises from the many competing demands impinging on them. Their struggles often lead them to seek psychotherapy. At the same time they often seek psychotherapy ambivalently. Maintaining therapy for these men involves delicately balancing their paradoxical desires. On the one hand seeking treatment is an acknowledgment of their need for interpersonal relatedness. However, they fear giving up their freedom when connected. These men characteristically avoid, withdraw, and isolate themselves from relationships, and as treatment develops, they may withdraw from this relationship, too. Monitoring the balance of their needs may forestall a premature retreat from psychotherapy. Conflicted bachelors' commitment to psychotherapy may be aided by clarifying and consistently re-acknowledging their specific goals for entering treatment.

Upon successful completion of his psychotherapy a bachelor will be able to accept his own needs for both interpersonal connectedness and independence without self-recrimination or social withdrawal. A bachelor's further ability to allow, express, act on, and satisfy his needs for social activities is another marker of successful growth. Forming positive relationships marked by increased levels of negotiation, mutuality, reciprocity, assertiveness, and interdependence will offer further behavioral affirmation of clinical change.

As a final comment about how to best benefit from psychotherapy, it may help to consider that the process can be enjoyable.

Redressing problems and fully engaging life—both facilitated within psychotherapy—can be quite delectable, certainly enchanting, often fun. Psychotherapy promotes dynamic people who entertain interesting prospects and implement them fully. Psychotherapy can support the important idea that life's glorious secrets and challenging mysteries are relatively simple, more dependent on vitally celebrating meaningful encounters than on procuring some trophy.

NOTES

1. This chapter makes suggestions to clients, particularly bachelors, about how they might best benefit from psychotherapy. Observations that address some of the specific challenges to therapists working with bachelors are summarized in C. A. Waehler. (1995). Relationship patterns of never-married men and their implications for psychotherapy. *Psychotherapy, 32,* 248–257.

2. Because this chapter is directed at the benefits bachelors can derive from psychotherapy, all references to clients are masculine. Of course, both men and women seek psychotherapy, and most of the general and specific guidelines suggested here are applicable to both sexes.

3. Two of the largest national organizations for psychotherapists, both of which have high ethical standards to which each member is accountable, are the American Psychological Association for psychologists and the American Counseling Association for counselors.

4. Not all psychotherapists, of course, are ideal. The guidelines presented here assume that you are seeing a knowledgeable and competent professional. This is not always the case. Sometimes it is in your best interest to be an informed consumer and not buy what a therapist is selling. Reflecting on your experiences in light of the guidelines here will help you evaluate the performance of an individual therapist so that you can be a more effective service consumer.

REFERENCES

Adams, M. (1981). Living singly. In P. Stein (Ed.), *Single life: Unmarried in social context* (pp. 221–234). New York: St. Martin's Press.

American Psychiatric Association. (1994). *Diagnostic and statistical manual of mental disorders* (4th ed.). Washington, DC: APA.

Bernard, J. (1972). *The future of marriage*. New Haven, CT: Yale University Press.

Blakeslee, S. (1991, August 28). Confirmed bachelorhood: It may be a state of mind. *The New York Times*, pp. C1, C10.

Cargan, L., & Melko, M. (1982). *Singles: Myths and realities.* Beverly Hills, CA: Sage Publications.

Darling, J. (1981). Later marrying bachelors. In P. Stein (Ed.), *Single life: Unmarried in social context* (pp. 34–40). New York: St. Martin's Press.

Davis, A., & Strong, P. (1980). Working without a net: The bachelor as a social problem. *Sociological Review, 25,* 109–130.

Erikson, E. (1950). *Childhood and society*. New York: Norton.

Gotlib, I., & McCabe, S. (1990). Marriage and psychopathology. In F. Fincham & T. Bradbury (Eds.), *The psychology of marriage: Basic issues and applications* (pp. 226–257). New York: Guilford Press.

Gove, W., Hughes, M., & Styles, C. (1983). Does marriage have positive effects on the psychological well-being of the individual? *Journal of Health and Social Behavior, 24,* 122–131.

Gubrium, J. (1975). Being single in old age. *International Journal of Aging and Human Development, 6,* 29–41.

Guntrip, H. (1969). *Schizoid phenomena, object-relations, and the self*. New York: International Universities Press.

Halligan, C. (1980). Neurosis and avoidant response as factors in non-marriage: A comparative study of never-married and married men. *Dissertation Abstracts International, 40*, 5811-B.

Hendrix, H. (1992). *Keeping the love you find: A guide for singles*. New York: Pocket Books.

Hughes, M., & Gove, W. (1981). Living alone, social integration, and mental health. *American Journal of Sociology, 87*, 48–75.

Jacoby, S. (1974, February 17). 49 million singles can't all be right. *The New York Times Magazine*, pp. 41–49.

Johnston, M., & Eklund, S. (1984). Life-adjustment of the never-married: A review with implications for counseling. *Journal of Counseling and Development, 6*, 230–236.

Kaplan, D., & Cohn, B. (1990, September 17). Presumed competent? *Newsweek, 116*, 32–33.

Kessler, R., & McRae, J. (1984). A note on the relationships of sex and marital status to psychological distress. *Research in Community and Mental Health, 4*, 109–130.

Levinson, D., Darrow, C., Klein, E., Levinson, M., & McKee, B. (1978). *Seasons of a man's life*. New York: Ballantine Books.

Mental health: Does therapy help? (1995, November). *Consumer Reports, 60*, 734–739.

Millon, T., & Everly, G. S. (1985). *Personality and its disorders: A biosocial learning approach*. New York: John Wiley & Sons.

Pearlin, L. I., & Johnson, J. S. (1977). Marital status, life strains, and depression. *American Sociological Review, 42*, 704–715.

Rallings, E. (1966). Family situations of married and never-married males. *Journal of Marriage and the Family, 28*, 485–490.

Robertson, M. (1974). The relationship between marital status and the risk of psychiatric referral. *British Journal of Psychiatry, 124*, 191–202.

Smith, M., Glass, G., & Miller, T. (1980). *The benefit of psychotherapy*. Baltimore: Johns Hopkins University Press.

Spreitzer, E., & Riley, L. (1974). Factors associated with singlehood. *Journal of Marriage and the Family, 36*, 533–542.

Stein, P. (1975). Singlehood: An alternative to marriage. *The Family Coordinator, 24*, 489–503.

————. (1978). The lifestyles and life changes of the never-married. *Marriage and Family Review, 1*, 1–11.

————. (Ed.). (1981). *Single life: Unmarried in social context*. New York: St. Martin's Press.

U.S. Bureau of the Census. (1993, March). *Current Population Reports* (Series P-20, No. 478, Marital Status and Living Arrangements). Washington, DC: U.S. Government Printing Office.

Waehler, C. (1991a). Selected Rorschach variables of never-married men. *Journal of Clinical Psychology, 47,* 123–132.

————. (1991b). Personality characteristics of never-married men. Poster presentation at the Annual Convention of the American Psychological Association, San Francisco.

————. (1992). Mid-life adjustment of never-married men. Paper presentation at the American Psychological Association, Washington, DC.

————. (1995). Relationship patterns of never-married men and their implications for psychotherapy. *Psychotherapy, 32,* 248–257.

Ward, R. (1981). The never-married in later life. In P. Stein (Ed.), *Single life: Unmarried in social context* (pp. 342–356). New York: St. Martin's Press.

————. (1979). The never-married in later life. *Journal of Gerontology, 34,* 861–869.

Winnicott, D. W. (1972). *Holding and interpretation.* New York: Grove Press.

FURTHER READING

Books that may be of interest in understanding bachelors are listed below.

Books that contemplate marriage or non-marriage from personal, psychological, or sociological perspectives include:

Carey, A. (1984). *In defense of marriage*. New York: Walker & Co.

Cargan, L., & Melko, M. (1982). *Singles: Myths and realities*. Beverly Hills, CA: Sage Publications.

Cate, R., & Lloyd, S. (1992). *Courtship*. Newbury Park, CA: Sage Publications.

Fincham, F., & Bradbury, T. (Eds.). *The psychology of marriage: Basic issues and applications*. New York: Guilford Press.

Gordon, T. (1994). *Single women: On the margins?* New York: New York University Press.

Levinson, D., Darrow, C., Klein, E., Levinson, M., & McKee, B. (1978). *Seasons of a man's life*. New York: Ballantine Books.

Schwartzberg, N., Berliner, K., & Jacob, D. (1995). *Single in a married world: A life cycle framework for working with the unmarried adult*. New York: Norton.

Stein, P. (Ed.). (1981). *Single life: Unmarried in social context*. New York: St. Martin's Press.

Books that aid individuals in their personal exploration and journey toward self-knowledge are available in widely divergent fields. Materials in this domain that may have special appeal to bachelors include:

Moore, T. (1992). *Care of the soul: A guide for cultivating depth and sacredness in everyday life*. New York: HarperPerennial.

Peck, M. Scott. (1979). *The road less traveled: A new psychology of love, traditional values and spiritual growth*. New York: Simon & Schuster.

Pirsig, R. (1974). *Zen and the art of motorcycle maintenance: An inquiry into values*. New York: William Morrow & Co.

Books that directly address areas in which bachelors sometimes desire personal development include:

Alberti, R., & Emmons, M. (1978). *Your perfect right: A guide to assertive behavior*. San Luis Obispo, CA: Impact Publishers.

Hendrix, H. (1988). *Getting the love you want: A guide for couples*. New York: HarperPerennial.

——— . (1992). *Keeping the love you find: A guide for singles*. New York: Pocket Books.

Malone, T., & Malone, P. (1987). *The art of intimacy*. New York: Simon & Schuster.

Books that further address some of the general psychological phenomena introduced in this text include:

Erikson, E. (1950). *Childhood and society*. New York: Norton.

Freud, S. (1909/1961). *Five lectures on psycho-analysis* (J. Strachey, Trans.). New York: Norton.

Guntrip, H. (1969). *Schizoid phenomena, object-relations, and the self*. New York: International Universities Press.

INDEX

About the Author

CHARLES A. WAEHLER is an Associate Professor in the Department of Psychology at The University of Akron, and a psychotherapist with Cornerstone Psychological Services in Akron, Ohio.